Praise for Elements

Climbers frequently struggle far more than necessary and for their tenacity I can't help but commend them but... there is an easier way! Elements of Rock Climbing opens the door to that 'easier way'.

Elements of Rock Climbing's approach to movement technique should prove very useful for neophyte climbers and serve as a helpful reminder for more experienced ones too. For some experienced climbers it will answer questions they didn't even consider. Good, solid information presented in a no-nonsense format.

The book presents the fundamentals of movement in a manner that can provide a solid foundation upon which to build. And without that foundation you will NEVER reach your climbing potential." ".....a wealth of useful information. It fills a gap that is increasingly found in climbers' knowledge.

Elements of Climbing contributes to the sport of climbing in two important ways. First, the subject matter provides easily digestible chunks of solid information that should serve all climbers well when it comes to moving on rock. Second, and at least as importantly, the explanations clearly communicate the excitement the author felt as he discovered the various principals discussed. It encourages people to go and try the subject matter on for size, and to expect positive results.

R L Stolz - owner of the climbing school Alpine Adventures in Keene Valley, New York

This book will make it easier for you to climb! In the past 20 years and after teaching thousands of people to climb, I have noticed that people excel reading about climbing concepts before trying to apply them. I found Elements of Rock Climbing, by Robert Burbank to be a complete, concise, description of climbing movement and techniques. The book also describes seldom mentioned, but very helpful concepts such as momentum! I recommend this book to the first time climber as well as the advanced beginner or intermediate looking to improve their climbing form.

Jay Foley owner of the climbing school Mountain Skills Climbing Guides New Mexico

Elements
of
ROCK
CLIMBING

Robert Burbank

Printed in the United States of America

Published by WingSpan Press, Livermore, CA

www.wingspanpress.com

The WingSpan name, logo and colophon are the trademarks of WingSpan Publishing.

First Edition 2010

ISBN 978-1-59594-382-8

Library of Congress Control Number: 2010926353

Dedication

To my parents for making me believe I could do anything I set my mind to.

To my wife Kathryn for her help in passing this same belief on to our children, for her love, and for her patience with me in supporting my various endeavors.

To my children; Carrie, Amy, and Tom, who are now fearlessly traveling on their own life quests.

To my grandchildren: Sarah, Lauren, Myles, Molly, and Kate, who are just now setting forth into the world...and learning that they too, can accomplish anything.

Preface

The book is aimed at the novice climber, the person who has climbed very little, or not at all. The book emphasizes the importance of using the brain to climb, rather than brute force. Novices tend to make an easy climb very difficult because they overlook, or don't know of, an easier way to climb. They select a hard move because they don't see the easy move.

Climbing books tend to focus on gear mechanics e.g. how to place gear, how to tie knots, etc. They tend to focus very little on how to actually climb. **This book's purpose is to illustrate how to climb.** Some general introductory climbing information is also included for the novice.

The book illustrates **how to use your hands and feet to move up the cliff using various combinations of push, pull, momentum, and balance.**

Table of Contents

Appendices

NOTICE

Although not covered in this book, **it is essential that you understand gear mechanics for safe climbing.** That is, you should learn how to use ropes, belaying devices, valid top rope setups, etc., in a manner that is safe for yourself, and for others.

Learning gear mechanics from a book cannot provide you with the training required for safe climbing. People who can climb well are not necessarily good teachers, and they may not understand safe gear mechanics. They, and their partners, may have been lucky up to now. For this reason, you **should receive proper training from a professional licensed guide before actually climbing.**

Chapter 1

Overview of Book Contents

Each chapter focuses on one or two main topics. Other issues are also selected out for emphasis. These particular issues range from general climbing concerns to recommendations on climbing problems.

An example of how they are exhibited is shown below.

Look Down—Use Your Feet

Novice climbers tend to spend most of their time looking up. Spend half your time looking down for holds. Use you feet to lift you up. Save your arm strength for when you need it.

Chapter Content

Chapter 1—Chapter Contents gives an overview of each chapter.

Chapter 2—Introduction to Climbing outlines what you need to begin climbing, finding partners, looking at partner safety, and other general information for the novice climber.

Chapter 3—Pulling Up and Highsteps are introduced by describing how they can be done using a set of stairs. This allows the reader to read how the move is done....and then make the move in a familiar environment. The requirements for making these moves, the problems associated with these moves on rock, etc., are also covered.

Chapter 4—Making Contact with the Rock introduces the new climber to various handholds, footholds, considerations of making contact with the rock, etc.

Chapter 5—Side Pulls, Laybacks, Stemming, and Barndooring expands on how to use side pulls to advantage. It also introduces Laybacks and Stemming. Problems associated with "Barndooring" are also discussed.

Chapter 6—More Contact with the Rock introduces new holds, smearing, using small footholds, and friction climbing. Thoughts on moving from hold-to-hold are also discussed.

Chapter 7—Cracks and Crack Climbing shows some of the holds associated with crack climbing....and identifies a few crack climbing issues for your consideration.

Chapter 8—Finding Rests and Swapping Hands and Feet emphasizes the importance of saving your strength and identifies a few ways to rest. Various ways to swap from one hand (or foot) on a hold to the other hand (or foot) are covered.

Chapter 9—Mantles and Roofs outlines various issues associated with mantles and moves following mantles. Roof considerations are also explored.

Chapter 10—Momentum and Dihedrals lists a number of ways to use momentum and some considerations regarding dihedrals.

Chapter 11—Summary / Conclusion summarizes the more important points in the book.

Appendices

Appendix I—The Climbing Process describes how climbers move up the cliff. It shows the steps used by the climber who leads, and the steps used by the climber who follows. Some of the more common climbing terms are introduced. Also describes the steps involved in the top rope process.

Appendix II—A Few Thoughts for the New Leader describes a number of considerations for the new leader to think about.

Appendix III—Analysis of Climbing Forces explores climbing situations by doing a rough calculation on the forces involved on the leg, the arm, and the body in various positions. It shows how the forces shift, as we change our climbing positions.

Appendix IV—Glossary of Terms

Chapter 2

Introduction to Climbing

I recommend that you skim through this book to see what it contains. Then, read again more slowly to absorb the information. You can then alternate back and forth...between reading the book, and climbing. If you are unfamiliar with the climbing process (the steps used and the more commonly used terms), the first thing you should do is read Appendix I—The Climbing Process.

A novice climber typically believes that climbing ability is a function of physical strength, flexibility and agility. Although these attributes are good to have as a climber, you need to know how to use, and combine, these abilities to strengthen your climbing skills. This book will help you in that area.

This chapter outlines some of the non-climbing information a novice will need. This includes: **(1) finding a partner, (2) evaluating a partner for safety, (3) a list of required climber gear/other, and (4) climb ratings.**

Two Primary Skills

Two primary skills you need as a climber are described in this book:

> ❖ **Making Contact with the Rock.** What are some of the ways to use a hold for achieving the push, or

pull, that you require? How should your feet, fingers, and hands grip the rock?

❖ **Combinations.** What are some of the ways of combining finger, foot, and hand rock contact with push, pull, balance, and momentum in a way that will move you up the rock face?

There are an infinite number of ways to hold, and move up the rock. This book shows commonly used, and some of the less commonly used, grips and combinations.

Frequently, there is more than one way to get through the same area of rock. The climber, when faced with an area of the rock that seems impossible, should **strive to believe that there is a way up**. And, since your partner just went up through that same area of rock (making it look easy), you have to believe there is a way up...You just have to find a solution.

Finding a Partner

If you are looking for a climbing partner and none of your friends or acquaintances climb, you might find someone at an indoor climbing wall, where you learn to climb, or at the cliff. Although, most of the cliffs require that you bring a partner, some cliffs have meeting places where climbers come without partners. I have found hundreds of partners at the cliff. Check with local climbers, climbing gear stores, the internet, etc., to determine if you can find partners at a particular climbing area.

When looking for a partner at the cliff, I walk up to people that are alone and ask them if they are looking for a partner. I describe my climbing ability. **It is important that you give an *accurate* description of your climbing ability.** An example of such a description might be: "I follow 9's and can go straight through 2/3's of the 10's. I am an 8 leader but have led a handful of 9's." This gives a fairly accurate description of your ability. Note that climb ratings will be discussed later in this chapter.

I have found climbing with new partners found at the cliff to be very interesting. Over the years, I have partnered with climbers from different U. S. states, Canada, European, Mid-Eastern, and South American countries. A number of these people became my regular partner.

Generally speaking, I have enjoyed meeting with, and climbing with, these new partners. They have been friendly and they have helped to make me a better climber. When I was a beginner (and described myself as such), I was surprised to find that high level climbers were very willing to climb with me.

A Safe Climbing Partner

A safe partner is essential...well trained and uses good judgment. The issue is how do you determine partner safety. This is not an easily solved problem. I usually ask potential partners about their climbing experience. If they can lead, then they probably (but not necessarily) are trained. The person who follows must ensure that the leader knows how to belay and how to set up a good anchor. There are other things that a leader can do that are unsafe, but most of these things endanger the leader, not the follower. (There are some things that can endanger the follower such as not providing adequate protection on a traverse.) When my partner takes the first lead, I watch how the rope is handled, how well gear is placed, how they set up their belay, etc. If I am going to take the first lead, I ask how experienced they are at belaying. I watch how they handle the rope, and how they tie into the rope. In addition, I check to make sure they have a nut tool to remove gear (to make sure they can remove gear...and, if they don't have a nut tool, it is an indicator that they are not experienced). I don't mind if a follower's gear skills are weak, as long as they are safe and they know how to remove protection gear from the rock. In addition, when I do the first lead, I select an easier climb, one I don't expect to fall on.

Top Roping Safety

If you are planning on top roping, one of you must be able to set up a safe top rope. This is not obvious, you have to know how to place gear that will hold, you need to have redundancy built in, and you need to know how to set up the slings and cords in a safe manner. I recommend that whoever sets up the top rope be trained by a professional licensed guide. If improperly set up, a combination of rope movement and weight on the rope can cut through the supporting slings/cords. This can lead to a fatality.

Partner Safety—Summary

I ask and observe as much as is practical. The more you know about climbing safety, the better you will be able to assess a partner...and the safer you and your partner will be. However, there are no guaranties, use good judgment to the fullest. If a question on safety arises, double-check it. This is not a sport for being shy about asking for clarification. If you don't understand something, ask questions until you do understand it.

Climbing Partner "Wants"

Assuming you have a safe partner, what more would you "want" from a partner. I look for someone who:

❖ Is pleasant, fun to climb with.

❖ Does not give "unrequested" advice.

❖ Does not waste a lot of time standing around while there is work to be done. (e.g., arranging rope, transferring gear, getting ready to climb, etc.). Climbers should not be racing to get ready to climb, but they also should not be standing around letting one person do all the preparatory work.

❖ Climbs 1-2 levels better than me if they plan to lead... and 1-2 levels less than me if they plan to follow. This allows both people to climb at their maximum level. However, climbing with people at any level is enjoyable.

What Do You Need to Start Climbing

I have been asked several times; What do you need to start climbing. Since you will not be leading in the beginning, you will need:

❖ **Enough training to make you: (1) a safe partner, and (2) able to assess your partner's safety skills.**

❖ **Climbing harness.**

❖ **Belay device.**

❖ **Nut tool and carabiner**....required if you are climbing at a location that uses traditional ("trad") gear protection. This is where cams, nuts, etc., are used for protection (as opposed to having bolts permanently fixed in the wall...called Sport Climbing). The carabiner can be used to attach your nut tool to your harness. Some climbers like to have the nut tool attached to the carabiner on a 12-18 inch length of cord to eliminate the chance of dropping the nut tool.

❖ **Climbing shoes.**

❖ **Climbing helmet.**

❖ **A set of Prusiks**...Two small loops of 5-6 mm cord (sold at climbing gear stores).

Prusiks can be used to climb up the rope should you fall and the rope you are hanging on isn't long enough to lower you to a ledge.

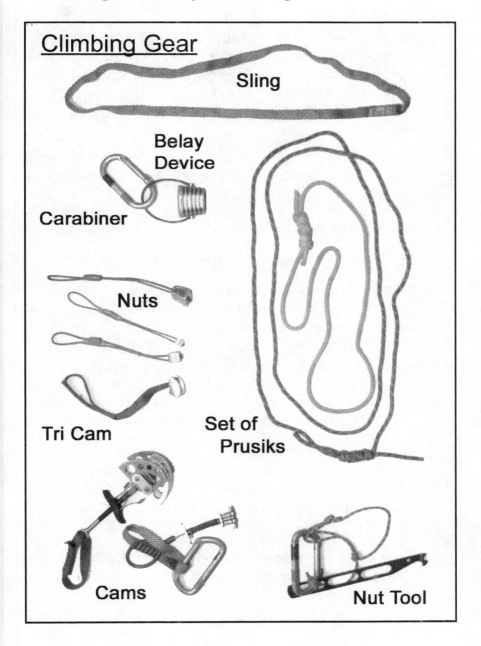

Climbing Gear

Sling

Belay Device

Carabiner

Nuts

Tri Cam

Set of Prusiks

Cams

Nut Tool

Prusiks can also be used to escape from a belay. This could be required should your leader fall and become incapacitated. Escaping from a belay should be learned from a professional licensed guide.

It should be noted that very few climbers carry Prusiks. Although I have used Prusiks only 3-4 times, I was extremely glad to have them. I believe they are important to carry. They are very light and inexpensive. They can be essential. Why not carry them?

They are difficult to use, but they do get you up the rope. It is best to learn how to use them before you need them.

"Nice-to-Have" Items

In addition you may want to add the following:

- ❖ **Chalk bag.** Some people might say that this is essential. It can be helpful if your fingers are wet from perspiration or on small/smearing holds. However, in my opinion, it is not essential for the novice climber who will be using larger holds. It tends to be way overused because people use it out of habit, or to build up their confidence in making a move. (Chalk is sometimes called "white courage.")

- ❖ **A Rope**. The leader usually has one rope. If you bring a second rope, you have the option of using two ropes when rappelling down. In addition, you can share rope usage, and rope cost, with your partner.

- ❖ **Two to three slings and three to four carabiners**. These can be very helpful when you want to tie into an anchor, etc.

❖ **A guidebook of the area where you plan to climb.** These books describe, and rate, the climbs.

❖ **More slings, anchoring devices, etc. if you plan to set up a top rope.** As mentioned previously, you or your partner must be trained to set up a safe top rope.

Keep an Open Mind

Keeping an open mind is very important. Doing so will allow you to discover new ways to make contact with the rock, create combinations, find rests, use your momentum, etc....doing so will make you a better climber

---

Introduction to Climb Ratings

Climbs are rated in area guidebooks. **Each climb is rated for difficulty.** The difficulty is determined by the area of the climb where the moves are most difficult. This is called the **crux** of the climb. In the U.S., climbs are rated for difficulty using the Yosemite Decimal System. Climbs that are difficult, but don't require a rope for safety, are rated "4" and climbs that are so difficult the climber must pull or step on gear (called Aid Climbing) are rated "6" (e.g., 6.0, 6.3, etc.).

This book is intended for climbs rated from 5.0 to 5.15. Originally climbers thought the most difficult climb that would ever be done would be rated a 5.9. However, as equipment and skills got better, it was found that climbs more difficult than 5.9 were being done. When this occurred, it was decided to go to 5.10 as the next step (which is a little confusing because, as a decimal, you would expect 5.10 to be equal to 5.1 and easier than 5.9. However, a 5.10 climb is one grade more difficult that a 5.9). This is read as "Five ten." The difficulty of climbing has now increased so that the range of difficulty ranges from 5.0 to 5.15.

My perception of difficulty is:

5.4 to 5.6	Beginner Climbs
5.7 to 5.9	Intermediate Climbs
5.10 to 5.12	Advanced
5.13 to 5.15	Professional

Climbs are also rated for difficulty/risk of placing gear while leading. These ratings are important to the person leading because it indicates the level of risk to the leader. Difficulty may be because there is no good place to insert protection. It can also be the result of an awkward, or difficult position, required by the leader to place protection.

As a beginner, *usually* the difficulty of placing protection gear does not impact you because you are following, not leading. However, as previously mentioned, there are certain situations where protection does impact the follower. A common one is following a long traverse with little, or no, gear installed (this is explained in more detail in Appendix II—A Few Thoughts for the New Leader). A good leader will protect the novice follower by avoiding such climbs...they will select another climb.

These ratings look like the movie ratings:

❖ "G"......Good protection, easy to place gear

❖ "PG"...Pretty good protection. These climbs may have an area where it is somewhat difficult to place gear....and the leader may have more space between gear than he/she would like.

❖ "R"......These climbs may have long stretches where it is difficult (or impossible) to place gear. It is **very dangerous** for a leader to fall in this situation. Leaders accepting this risk should feel very competent leading "R" rated sections.

❖ "X"......These climbs offer little opportunity to place gear. There are one or more sections that are **extremely dangerous** for the leader. Anyone accepting the risk of leading these sections should be extremely competent climbing at the level of the X-rated section. This rating indicates a risk similar to climbing without a rope.

Climbs are also rated for quality. Climbs are sometimes given stars (e.g., 1, 2, or 3) to indicate that they have interesting moves, don't have large sections of uninteresting areas, clean/no dirt, etc. The more stars the better. Only the best climbs get one or more stars.

Ratings—Summary. The validity of climb ratings is as good as the person doing the rating. For the most part, the rating of one climb relative to another, for a given guidebook, is usually good. However, some climbing areas have climbs rated somewhat easier, or more difficult, than another area. 5.8's in one area may be as difficult as 5.7's in another area. Be cautious when beginning a new area.

Look for Holds Under Overhangs

It is not uncommon for climbers to miss a foothold that is directly below their waist and between their legs...particularly, where there is a waist-high overhang, or bulge. In this situation, the bulge or overhang can hide the foothold. The foothold may not be visible unless you lean out a little. These footholds can frequently be used as highsteps. Sometimes you can use them with no hands.

Note: For the purpose of discussion, when the word "grip" is used it applies to all holds used by finger, hand, or foot....and those used for pulling, as well as those that can be used for pushing.

Chapter 3

Pulling Up and Highsteps

A **Familiar Climbing Example.** In order to understand how to move up the rock, it may be helpful to consider how we move in a more common situation...such as moving up stairs. Analyzing movement up stairs may seem unimportant. However, doing so will allow you to experience and analyze various moves used in rock climbing. Making these moves on stairs, and analyzing them, will make it easier for you to make similar moves on rock.

After reading how to do each of the three following moves, do them on the stairs. Note how you lift your body up, how you balance, and how much arm or leg pull is required. Try the moves using one stair higher than described and one step lower than described. Consider how much your arms are lifting you up....and how much your legs are lifting you up.

Pulling Up—Facing Cliff

Standing at the bottom of the stairs, place your right foot on the third stair and grab handrails with your hands. Then, simultaneously pull the handrails and straighten your right leg. Your arm pull and legs have moved your body up the stairs. Your center of gravity is over your feet.

Note that this move is not what is commonly called a "pull-up" (where you lift with arms only).

Pulling Up—90 Degrees to Cliff

Face the stairs and turn 90 degrees to the right. You are now sideways to the stairs with your left side closest to the stairs. Place your left foot on the third stair. Reach up with your left hand, grab the right hand rail, and pull yourself up. You have now pulled yourself up with one hand and one foot....The other hand and foot are free to move to new holds. This is a very important move in climbing. This move is used frequently and is something you should consider when you can't find a good handhold above you.

Highstep

Place your right foot on the second stair, lean your body forward so that your center of gravity is directly over your right foot. At this point, your right leg is bent. Balance yourself on this leg. Place your hands on the handrails for safety. Then, while maintaining balance, slowly straighten your bent right leg. You have now moved your body up the stairs with no appreciable use of arm pull. You now have your center of gravity over your feet. Straightening your right leg did all the lifting.

Side Pull Grip

You can pull up using a side pull in the same manner you do on a hold that is above you. In the example above, you pulled on a railing. When on rock, you can do a side pull from a single vertical edge. Additional data on side pulls can be found in Chapter 5.

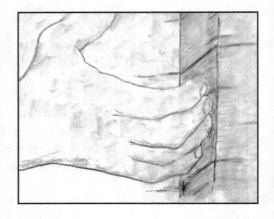

Pulling Up—Requirements

❖ A foothold.

❖ A fairly good handhold, one that is good enough to provide the force you need...in the direction you need....as you straighten your leg.

Trouble, Try Another Method

Each climber has a unique set of skills and physical attributes. A solution that fits one climber may not fit another.

Climber differences are obvious (e.g., some climbers will be able to reach very high, some climbers can stretch their feet very wide, etc.) and not-so-obvious (arm/torso length, body position, angle of pull, location of center of gravity, etc.).

If a method used by another climber doesn't work, try to find a way that will work. Most climbers are stubborn (being a little stubborn is not a bad thing). There comes a time to try another method.

Pulling Up—Considerations

❖ Pulling up is the first thing (and sometimes the last thing) a novice climber thinks of using. It is also used frequently by every level of climber.

❖ The disadvantage of this move is that it requires a fair amount of arm and leg force.

❖ A foothold to step up on.

❖ A handhold that will provide the force you need...in the direction you need...to move your body's center of gravity over your leg. The force required may be minimal.

Highstep—Tall Climber Advantage

Tall climbers usually have an advantage in doing highsteps. It is easier to step on a foothold that is waist high, than one that is two to three inches above waist high. In addition, because a tall person's center of gravity is high, it requires less arm pull because the center of gravity is almost directly over the foot.

(Note: There are climbs that have a crux easier for a short person....I like to take my tall friends on these.)

Highstep—Requirements

❖ A foothold to step up on.

❖ A handhold that will provide the force you need....in the direction you need...to move your body's center of gravity over your leg. The force required may be a lot, a little, or none.

❖ The ability to stand up on your bent leg after you have moved your center of gravity over your foot.

Highstep—Considerations

This is a very useful and frequently used move.

Highsteps can be broken into two basic situations:

❖ One, where the hold is in such a position that you can balance over it with *little or no use of your arms,* (e.g., below your waist at knee-high level). Also, if the hold is not too high, and it is not too far away, you can "rock up onto your foot" by using a small hop...or lunge.

"Rock onto your foot"

❖ Two, where the hold is off to the side or up so high that *significant force* is required to move your center of gravity over your foot. (Try doing Highstep Example on page 16 and place foot on the 4th step rather than on the 2nd step.)

In both cases your foot lifts your body up. In situation one, you use little or no arm force. In situation two, you use significant arm force.

More commonly however, you will be faced with situation two. There are three steps required to complete a situation two highstep:

❖ one, placing the foot on the hold

❖ two, moving your center of gravity over your foot

❖ three, straightening your bent leg

An analysis of each of these three steps is outlined below.

Highstep—Placing the Foot on the Hold

Sometimes when doing a highstep, the foot is easily placed on the hold. At other times, it is extremely difficult (e.g., when the hold is close to the body and very high up). Some climbers can place their foot on a very high hold because of their excellent flexibility. When the hold is high, but somewhat away from you, it may be helpful to lean back away from the hold. This allows you to lift your foot higher.

If you plan to place the toe end of your foot on the hold, you want to place your foot on the hold as flat as possible. This will mean that you have to point and push down the toe end of your foot as far as you can. If you can't use the toe end of your foot, you might be able to use your heel on the hold. As you move your center of gravity over your body you will have to reposition your foot.

Highstep—Moving Your Center of Gravity over Your Foot

Moving your body over your foot can be difficult. It can sometimes require a lot of force...and sometimes a lot of finesse. If you keep your knee bent, it will require less strength to move your body over your foot. Moving your body over your foot can be accomplished using an unlimited number of combinations. You can combine such things as arm pull, arm push, foot push, and momentum (e.g., a lunge..."rock on up over your foot"). Sometimes you move your body part way using an arm or leg...and then you have to find another hold to go the rest of the way. Hopefully, another hold can now be reached to help you complete the movement. When you are almost balanced, you require very little force to move your body the last few required inches. Even an extremely small vertical edge (one too small to get your fingers on) can be used by pushing a fingernail (in line with your fingers) against the edge. Also, you may find a hold on the other side of your body you can use to push yourself horizontally.

Highstep—Straightening Your Bent Leg

Again, it may be easy to straighten your leg when you are

balanced over your foot. You may be able to just straighten your leg, or you may be able to reach a foot- or handhold that will assist you to straighten your leg.

However, it may also be extremely difficult to straighten your leg when you can't find foot- or handholds to help you. In this situation, it may be possible to assist your effort by placing a hand on your knee and pushing down. This may be enough to allow you to stand up on the bent leg.

Another way that may work is to "lunge." Try to straighten your leg with a lunging thrust and lock off your knee. You may have gained a few inches. Thrust again, and lock off your knee. The higher you go the easier it gets.

Stemming

Stemming is another move used a lot in climbing. It involves pushing against two holds usually done with the feet spread wide apart and pushing into the wall. You can stem using very small holds or even smooth walls because your feet are pushed into the wall face, sometimes with a lot of force. You can also stem using two arms. Stemming can be particularly useful for resting and it is the predominant move in climbing dihedrals.

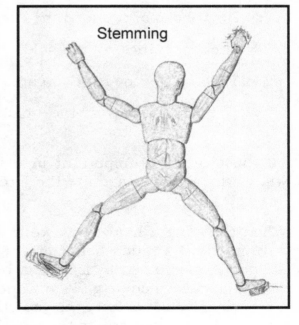
Stemming

Chapter 4

Making Contact with the Rock

Make Maximum Use of Holds. For All contact with the rock, it is very important to maximize the use of the rock. You should be determining by sight and feel:

❖ The size of the hold.

❖ How sharp or rounded the edges.

❖ The smoothness of the hold.

❖ The angle of the rock you are gripping.

❖ The relationship of the hold....to the direction of force you require.

All these are very important in determining if the grip will work...and to maximize the force you will be able to generate.

When grabbing a hold, move your hand around a little. You may find a much better grip. Some of these factors are determined better by feel, than by sight. Frequently, a very small movement (e.g., ¼ to ½ inch sideways) will yield a significantly better hold. As you climb, you will become better at fitting your grip to the rock. Using good holds will become automatic.

Hold Examples

- ❖ **Jug**. This is the hold that fits your hand like a baseball bat....You can wrap your fingers around it. This hold is as good as it gets.

- ❖ **Four Finger-wide Ledge**. This hold is big enough to get all four fingers over the edge. Three ways to do this are:

  - ➤ **Finger tip pads over edge without support of thumb**. This is usually used if you can't reach high enough to engage your thumb.

  - ➤ **Finger tip pads on ledge with thumb wrap around support**. Note that the fingers are pressed together for support. In addition, the thumb supports the fingers in two ways: one, by pressing against the fingers so that they act as a single grip, and two, the top half of the thumb's first joint is slightly wrapped around the first finger.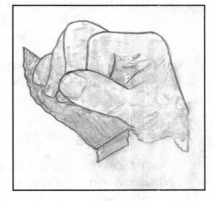

  - ➤ **Tips of four fingers on edge supported by thumb.** This hold tends to be used when the edge is small and isn't deep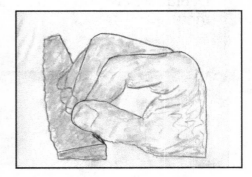

enough to lay your fingers on it in an effective manner.

Note that, although the thumb is not wrapped around the fingers, it is pushing hard against the side of the first finger for support...and that all fingers are squeezed together to act as a single unit.

Selecting Holds

Plan ahead. Before selecting a hold to use, consider your next move. Can you see holds that will support further movement? Will the hand you need be free after you move up? Should you move so that the other hand will be free?

Hang straight armed. As you are looking for holds, hang straight armed. This leaves your weight on your skeleton frame....not your arm muscles. Novice climbers tend to hang from bent arms. Save your strength for when you need it.

Don't move off a hold until you know where you plan to go. Novices tend to move a hand/foot off a hold before considering where it should go. They leave a foot hanging in the air looking for a place to put it down. This wastes arm and finger strength. Decide where you want a foot (or hand) to go...*then* move it.

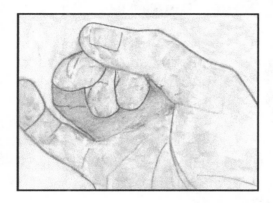

❖ **One, two and three finger-wide ledge holds.**
Similarly, holds that will allow only one, two, or
three fingers can be grabbed with as many fingers
as there is room... and the thumb and other fingers
can provide support. Note how the fingers and
thumb provide support.

❖ **Pinch Grip**. A pinch grip allows you to use one or
more fingers to pinch the rock with your thumb. ...
and can be used to pull, push, or, if you are strong
enough, pull you up. A pinch grip can be a key factor
in keeping your body from peeling away from the
cliff, while the main part of the force you are using
comes from your other arm and from your feet.

Small Steps Better than Big Ones

It takes less effort to take small steps than it does to
take big ones. When small easy steps are available,
use them...rather than taking one big step.

Save arm and leg strength for when you really need
it.

Foothold—Shoe Inner Edge. The shoe's inner edge is frequently used. It is very effective on narrow edges. Your climbing shoe edge should make contact with the hold right next to the top joint of the first toe. Your weight should be carried on that same toe joint. It helps if, while weighting your foot, you: (1) turn your ankle into the cliff somewhat (lifting the outside edge of your foot up slightly), and (2) lift your large toe up as much as possible.

When the hold is larger, you can place more of your shoe on the ledge allowing your weight to be more evenly distributed over your foot.

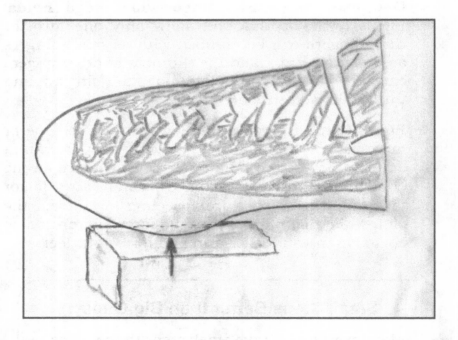

Foothold—Outside of the Foot. Although the outside edge of the foot is not used as often as the inside edge, it is useful. One such use is when you alternate between: (1) stepping up with the outside foot edge, and (2) stepping up with the inside foot edge. Because this looks like a figure from Egyptian Hieroglyphics, it is also called the "Egyptian."

Foothold—Toe. The toe can also be used on holds to advantage. (e.g., it can allow you to reach a hold by standing up on your toe). In addition, sometimes a hold can be situated where it is difficult to utilize a foot edge but can be used by the toe. This occurs sometimes when the hold is directly in front of you and you cannot move to the side.

Handhold Other—Walking Fingers over Edge. Sometimes a hold is just out of reach, but you can get your fingertips on the edge of the hold. When this occurs, you may be able to "walk" your finger tips over the hold. Although your arm can't stretch far enough on its own, it can sometimes be pulled a short distance.....allowing you to grab the hold.

Chapter 5

Side Pulls, Laybacks, Stemming, and Barndooring

Side pulls. One of the most useful holds (and one most often overlooked by novice climbers) is the side pull. The side pull can use a vertical rock edge...one that allows a horizontal pull (or push). The side pull was introduced in Chapter 3–page 16 where it is shown and described. It may, or may not, allow any downward pull. Side pulls can also be achieved using pinch grips, cracks, etc.

Using a side pull

The side pull can be used with a foothold that is on the same side of your body as the side pull. This was demonstrated in Chapter 3 using stairs as an example "Pulling Up—90 Degrees to Cliff". This is the same movement you make on a "Pull Down,", except it is 90 degrees to the wall. One advantage of making this move is that it can be done using only one arm and one leg. The other leg and arm are free to make the next move. In addition, the hold need not be above you. You can make this move by pulling horizontally on your arm.

When you can't find a hold to pull you up, you should look for an edge or another hold you can use as a side pull. If you find a side pull, look for a foothold that will work with the side pull.

Laybacking

Laybacking is the term for simultaneously:

❖ Leaning away from a hold as you pull on it.

❖ Pushing with your foot in a direction opposite of the direction your arm is pulling

When you layback in this manner your foot *pushes* and your arm *pulls* to keep you in position.

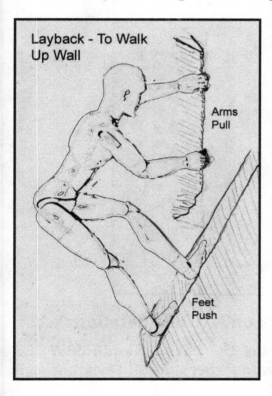

Layback - To Walk Up Wall

Arms Pull

Feet Push

Laybacking can be used to make one single movement up the cliff, or it can be done with a series of arm pulls and foot pushes that allow you to "walk" up a wall face with your feet. The force created by your arm pull can generate enough foot friction for you to walk up an almost vertical wall. This usually requires a fair amount of arm force.

Laybacking can be used to walk up a rockface. This walking can be done in a horizontal direction, a vertical direction, or anything in between. To move up a crack, walk your feet and arms up the crack... one limb at a time. Sometimes when the crack is vertical (or near vertical), the arms are pulling close to horizontal. The higher the feet, the more strenuous the pull is on the arms. If you can keep your feet somewhat below your arms as you walk them up, you can reduce the stress on your arms.

Laybacks can also be used to traverse or move horizontally if you have an edge, undercling or other handholds that will allow you to pull while "walking your feet horizontally.

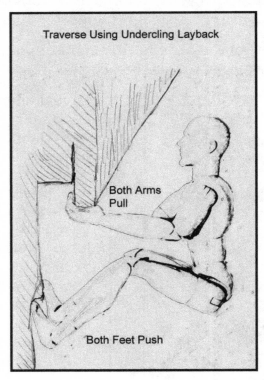

Traverse Using Undercling Layback

Both Arms Pull

Both Feet Push

Which Side to Layback on?...Considerations

❖ **Which side provides the better handholds?** i.e. Does one side have sharper edges? Does one side have rounded edges?

❖ **Which side provides better footholds?** i.e. Does one side extend out a little...leaving room for footholds?

Is one side rougher than the other? Does one side have any edges you can step on?

❖ **The angle of the crack as it runs up the face.** The more the crack angles like a ramp, the more weight you can place on your feet and the less force you will put on your arms.

❖ **The slope of the wall face.** If it is overhanging somewhat, there may be a tendency to peel away from the cliff. One side may be less likely to cause this to happen...One side may have holds you can use to avoid peeling away from the cliff.

❖ **Are there any holds near the crack** that you might use for a foot or handhold?

❖ **How will you exit from the layback?** Because laybacking is strenuous, you will want to determine how you will move out of the layback position....and return to face climbing. It may be easier to exit from one side of the layback than the other.

Changing Sides when Laybacking

Occasionally you will find yourself on the wrong side of a layback...wishing you were laybacking from the other side. In addition, there may be no hold that you can use to move to the other side. When this occurs, you may be able to use momentum to move to the other side. You may be able to throw yourself to the other side while twisting your foot (or changing feet).....and rapidly catching yourself in a layback on the other side. A rapid transfer from one side to the other will help to keep you from peeling away from the cliff.

This technique can be used when you are laybacking a crack or any other handhold.

Side Pulls—Peeling from Cliff

Side Pulls can help you from peeling away from the cliff by...pulling you into the cliff as you pull horizontally. The friction generated by your side pull allows some inward pull toward the cliff.

Barndooring

One problem with using side pulls is the possibility of "barndooring". Barndooring occurs when you are gripping the rock with one foot and one hand....and your body is pulling you away from the cliff. Your body swings out like a barn door on hinges.

Some of the techniques that can be used to avoid barndooring:

- ❖ **Lean your whole body as close to the rock as possible...*particularly the inside of the shoulder*** that is doing the pulling. Twist your body *and push that shoulder right into the rock*. In addition, while keeping your body close to the cliff, bend *away* from where your foot is pushing and your arm is pulling.

- ❖ **Place the foot you are pushing as far from the cliff as possible. If** your foot is on a ledge, place it on the outside as far as it will go.

- ❖ **The unweighted outer leg can be extended out straight alongside the rock face**

- ❖ The extended foot pushing sideways against the cliff can stop the barndooring.

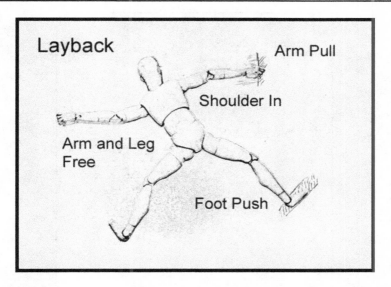

- ❖ **Use a hand, finger, or foothold to keep from barndooring.** Even a small amount of force provided by gripping a small nub or a very thin edge may enough.

Flagging

Sometimes when your weighting only one foot and you are in a situation where you could possibly fall off balance... or where your body might twist away from the wall, it helps to place the unweighted foot against the wall as a steadying factor. This is called "flagging". Very little force is involved; simply touching the wall may provide the stability you need. One example of flagging is mentioned above in barndooring. Flagging is also helpful in other delicate balance situations.

Flagging examples

- ❖ Placing the right foot out to the left...touching the toe or side of the foot against the wall.

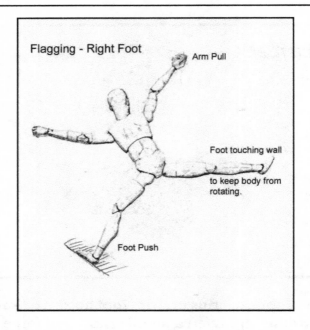

❖ Placing the left foot around behind your body touching your foot to the wall on your right.

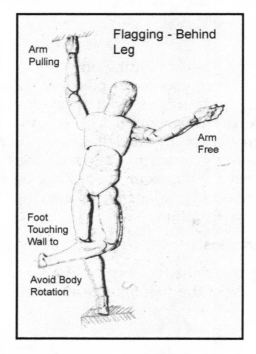

❖ Inserting your left foot between your body and the wall allowing you to touch the wall on the right with your left foot. This is more commonly done when you are kneeling.

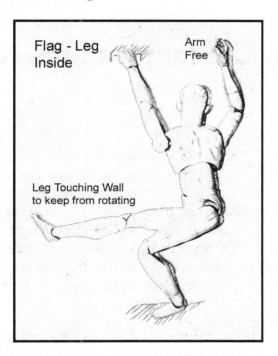

Flag - Leg Inside

Arm Free

Leg Touching Wall to keep from rotating

Use Alternate Foot and Hand
for Maximum Reach

For maximum reach, you should use the arm that is opposite the foot you are standing on. That is, if you are standing on your left foot, you use the right arm to stretch for the hold. (and similarly, stretch with your left arm when standing on your right leg). You can reach higher utilizing opposite arm/leg combinations than you can utilizing same side combinations.

Chapter 6

More Contact with the Rock

Friction **Holds/Smearing** Friction holds are ones that rely on friction alone to "grab" the rock...where there is nothing to actually grab, pinch, or wedge. Using friction holds is also called "smearing." You can smear with your hands and your feet. When you smear, you want as much of your foot or hand in contact with the rock as possible. This will generate the maximum amount of friction. Your climbing shoes have no tread to maximize friction.

Using friction holds requires that you generate a force into the wall where the hand (or foot) is smearing the wall. The more force into the rock, the more resultant friction. This can be observed by pushing a shoe across the floor with your finger...easy to do when empty but difficult to do with someone standing in the shoe. If you want to generate a lot of friction, find a way to apply force into the wall. When you are smearing in a standing position, try to keep your weight directly over your feet. Note: There is a tendency to want to lean toward the wall...if you lean and push into the wall you will push your foot away from the wall with an equal amount of force...making it more likely that your foot will slip.

As described in Chapter 5, you can generate the force necessary for the required friction using laybacks. Also, you can use body positions as described later on in this chapter: "Pushing into the Rock with Your Feet." When the rock angle isn't too high, and/or the rock is rough enough, it is possible to step up the rock without using your hands.

When smearing, you should look for potential footholds where the rock face is less than vertical (i.e., a scooped out area) and where the rock has the roughest surface. A scooped out area will allow you to place more weight on your feet and make it more likely that your foot won't slip.

Rounded and mounded areas (e.g., rock shaped like the top of a large bowling ball) can be used by placing the hand on the top of the hold with the fingers widespread to make maximum friction with your palm and fingers. You can pull on the mounded area without actually grabbing it (this assumes you do not have a hand large enough to actually grab the hold). If the hold is above you, you can pull somewhat on this type of hold. Even though you cannot really grab the hold, the friction from the arm pull can keep the hand on the hold. This hold may not generate a lot of pull force, but it may be enough.

Friction holds may be used with other holds when you are face climbing. In addition, there are climbs where the cliff is at a low angle such that climbing can be done using almost all friction holds. These climbs are called "friction climbs".

It should be noted that friction holds can be used in most of the combinations that exist.......they can be used for a highstep, for stemming, for mantels, etc. Using friction to hold the rock is also mentioned in crack climbing.

Three Finger Inside Corner Hold

When pulling from a 90 degree (or so) cut in the rock, it may help to place your first three fingers in a triangular shape stacking them behind the second finger. This particular 3-finger hold is displayed as viewed from inside the hold. This hold can be very effective when it is pulled downward, and diagonally, toward the climber...forcing the fingers into the corner. You may also be able to wrap your thumb around your first finger to provide even more strength.

Using Arm Push to Lift Foot

Sometimes it is helpful to lift your foot up to a new hold by pushing down on a hold with a hand. A hold that can be used for this purpose is usually at a height between knee high and shoulder high... and it is on the same side as the leg you are lifting. Pushing down on the hand takes the weight off the foot allowing you to move your foot to another hold. Also, in this situation, the best place to move your foot to...may be the same hold that the hand is using to push down on. See figure.

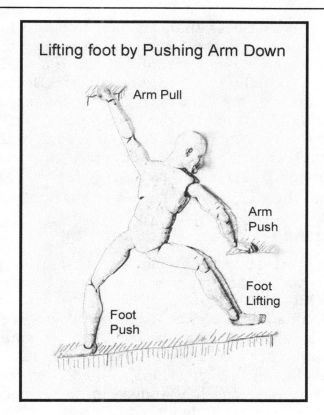

Lifting foot by Pushing Arm Down

Undercling Hold

Underclings occur on the underside of roofs, cracks, overhangs, and regular holds. Underclinging holds are those that you grab with your hands facing upward. You force your fingers up into a crack, a hole, an edge, or behind something you can grab. Underclings are frequently found where two walls come together (i.e., where the underside of a roof, or overhang, meets the vertical wall).

Even if there is no crack, edge, or nub to use, you may still be able to undercling the underside of a flat ledge using the friction generated by the upward push of your hands.

One common source of undercling holds comes from "flakes"). A flake is stone that looks like it is peeling, or "flaking" away from the rock face. Flakes come in all sizes, from small (less than an inch thick) to large (100 feet wide and one to two feet thick). They may be shaped like a thin dinner plate partially stuck to a wall, a piece of plywood partially stuck to the wall, etc. Before pulling on, or underclinging a flake, it is a good idea to assess (to the extent you can) if your planned force on the flake will pull the flake off the wall......and what will happen should this occur. Flakes are frequently used in climbing and although I have never personally seen a flake break away from the cliff, it does happen occasionally.

Combination—Other...Push and Pull

Another combination that can be used is to push on one leg while pulling on the other leg in a manner that helps to lift your body up. Although this combination is used infrequently, it can be useful when you are under a roof. Usually when using this combination, your body is somewhat higher than horizontal (i.e., your shoulders are somewhat higher than your hips). Your top leg reaches out for a way to pull (possibly wedged in a crack or a flake), and your bottom leg finds a hold below the pulling foot to push against. This combination of pushing and pulling will create a force that will lift your body somewhat.

If Only Room for One Hand, Grab Wrist

If you need to pull up and there is room for only one hand, grab the hold with the right hand and grab your right wrist with your left hand. You can then use both arms to pull up.

40

Footholds—Small/Rounded Foothold

Usually the best way to step on a small hold is to place the inside of the climbing shoe on the small rock edge at the point next to where the largest toe is joined to the foot. This is described in Chapter 4. Even if the hold is small (1/8 to 1/4 inch), you should be able to place all, or most of your of weight, on the hold. When the hold is very narrow and/or rounded, it sometimes helps if you roll your foot onto the hold as you weight your foot.

Pushing into the Rock with Your Feet

When using a foothold on a very small hold, or a smear hold, it is usually better (and sometimes necessary) that your foot is forced *into* the wall. The force pushing your foot into the wall can keep your foot on the hold. Your body position can help to create a force that pushes your foot into the wall.

The figure on the next page shows a climber holding some of the body weight on the arms and some of the weight on the feet. Notice that the climber and the rock face make a triangle. The forces can be described in general terms as follows:

❖ The arms are pulling the body *upward and into* the cliff.

❖ The feet are pushing *downward and away* from the cliff.

❖ The weight of the climber is held up by the *sum of the direct vertical pull of the arms and the direct vertical push of the feet.*

❖ The *direct horizontal pull of the arms is equal to the direct horizontal push of the feet* into the cliff. (This horizontal push into the cliff helps to keep your foot on the hold.)

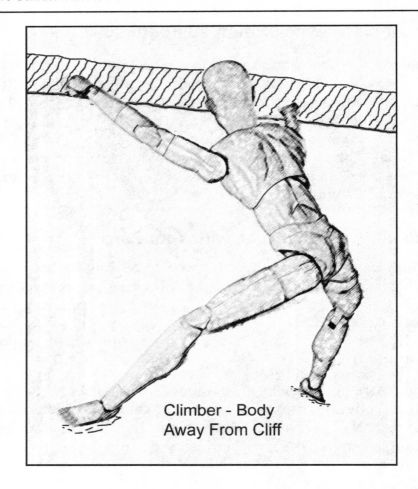

Climber - Body
Away From Cliff

❖ *The forces are a function of your body weight and the angles that your arms and feet have with the cliff.* These angles change as you move your waist away from the cliff.

❖ *A climber with the waist further from the cliff generates more horizontal foot force into the wall.* This improves the chances that a smear hold will work, but it also generates more arm pull, making it a more strenuous position.

❖ *A climber closer to the cliff reduces the pull on the*

arms, but also reduces the horizontal push of the feet into the wall. Your feet are more likely to slip off a very small hold as you experience less horizontal force pushing your foot into the cliff.

Although a general understanding may be helpful, it is not necessary to analyze forces on the arms and legs. As you climb, you will gain an intuitive understanding of the forces involved, and you will learn how to adjust your body position to fit the situation at hand with no apparent thought...much as you might do when you ride a bike.

For those interested, a more detailed analysis of climbing forces can be found in the Appendix III- Analysis of Climbing Forces.

Heel Hooking

Heel hooking occurs when you swing your leg up, and onto, a ledge or on a hold. The heel hooking helps by taking part of your body weight away from your arms. This hold can be very useful when you are trying to go over a roof. In addition, it can be used to help you traverse laterally on a roof ledge...hopefully, to a place where a hold can be reached that will allow you to pull yourself higher.

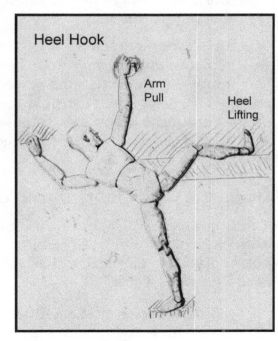

Chapter 7

Cracks and Crack Climbing

C racks can be used as just another method of finding a grip on the rock...They can be used in conjunction with other holds as you face climb or friction climb.

Cracks can also be used as the main pathway of a climb. You work your way up the crack primarily using holds that a crack provides.

When climbing a crack, it is not uncommon for a climber to completely miss a very good hold. This occurs because the climber is concentrating on the crack, he/she misses the good hold on the face next to the crack. Don't get so engrossed in the crack that you overlook holds on the face next to the crack...or even some good holds on the inside of the crack walls.

Using the Crack for Gripping the Rock

The first step in climbing a crack is the same as climbing all rock, look for holds. When looking for a hold in a crack you should first assess how wide the crack is. The following holds may be useful:

❖ **Finger Jams** are useful in narrow cracks. To use one, find a way to wedge one or more fingers in a crack. For example, the first three fingers in the crack can be inserted either thumb up or thumb down, whichever feels better. (I tend to prefer thumb down...but, that is just my personal preference.) To use three fingers with the thumb down, you insert the fingers and twist your wrist down to force your fingers against the sides of the crack. If the crack narrows below your fingers, it is also helpful if you can wedge

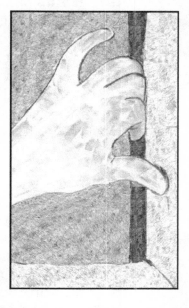

your fingers *downward* into the crack. If possible, you should also bring your thumb into play...either by wrapping it in some manner around your fingers or pushing it against the rock face to help lock your fingers in place.

Grips Change As You Move Up

As you move your body up, the grip on a hold may get better.....or it may get worse.

A ledge that you can pull on, but cannot grab, may be a good hold to pull down on, but as you move up it will tend to get worse.

As you pull yourself up over a small, smeared foothold, your body becomes more vertical and the hold gets worse.

❖ **Ring Holds** can be used for narrow cracks that are too wide for finger jams. Finger ring holds can be used where a crack narrows to about one half to one inch or so. Insert your fingers and thumb separately in the crack, wrap the fingers and the thumb in a circle around the area that narrows. With the thumb hooked over the end of the two fingers (on the fingernails), you can now pull.

❖ **Hand Jams** can be used for cracks that are too wide for fingers. You should use the widest part of your hand near your wrist as a wedge. The hand is made as narrow as possible with your thumb, palm, and fingers all flat as possible and in the same vertical plane. This hand is placed in line with the crack, wedged in as much as possible, and then, the thumb is brought down toward the fingers to force the bottom thumb/palm muscle to become wider... bringing pressure against the sides of the crack. Cupping the hand may also be helpful. Again, finding the best placement for the hand jam is critical.

❖ **Fist Jams** can be used in medium-sized cracks. Narrow your hand by placing your thumb joint under your palm as far as it will go. Your hand is now as wide as the four knuckles of your hand. Place the horizontal hand in the crack (hopefully in an area that is slightly slotted), and make a fist. This will push your thumb sideways and make your hand wider...and put pressure against the sides of the crack.

❖ **Foot Jams** are utilized in a manner similar to how fingers and hands are jammed. The foot can be:

➢ Turned on edge, and inserted in crack, with the knee raised to lock the foot in place. See figure.

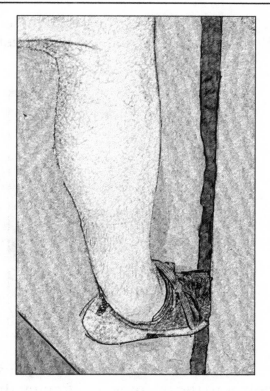

> ➤ Flat with toe directly into the crack.

> ➤ Flat with heel and toe across the crack.

❖ A wider crack can be jammed using both feet by forming a "T" with the heel of one foot against the inside of the middle of the other foot.

❖ **Arm Bars** can sometimes be used in wider cracks. An arm bar can be achieved by inserting an arm in a crack and pushing the hand against one side of the crack inner face...and the elbow or upper arm against the other inner face.

❖ **Knee Bars** can be used in wider cracks by inserting horizontally a leg and: (1) pushing your foot against one side of the crack, and (2) pushing the knee (and just above the knee) against the other side of the crack. This is similar to the method used in the arm bar. Pressure can be achieved by pushing on the ball of your foot.

❖ A knee bar variation can be used by inserting a leg vertically into the opening and forcing the side of the foot against one inner face, and the opposite side of the knee against the other inner wall. Pressure can be achieved by twisting your leg to the side.

Using the Best Part of a Crack

Deciding what part of the crack to use should be based on two things:

❖ What part of the crack will provide the best grip on the rock.

❖ What part of the crack is the best location for providing the direction of pull, or push, that you need.

You sometimes have to compromise and not use the

best hold because it doesn't provide the directional pull or push you require.

You should assess the crack and try to determine where the grip will work best:

❖ Where does the crack narrow down?

❖ Where does the crack widen as you go into it?

❖ Where can you press your thumb against a wall face as you lock your fingers in place?

❖ Is there a hold on the inside of the crack that can be used in some manner by foot or hand?

❖ Is any part of the crack rough, an area that will provide better friction for a jam?

Note that although these "jamming" holds are described for use in a crack, many of them can also be used between two regular holds, or in a horizontal indentation in the rock.

Chapter 8

Finding Rests
Swapping Hands/Feet

Finding Rests

You should keep your fingers and arms reasonably rested when you can, and save your strength for when you need it. If possible, you will want to rest before, during, and after a difficult section. As you approach a difficult area, you should determine if there is a way to rest while going through, and after going through, this difficult area. This may incent you to rest more before beginning the difficult area. Some of the ways to rest have been mentioned before, but they are worth repeating. They are:

* ❖ **Finding an area of the cliff that is somewhat less than vertical**...A place where you can stand using your hands for balance only. You may be able to find a way to rest using no hand. You may be able to rest while leaning into the cliff with your arms hanging down.

* ❖ **Stemming (introduced in Chapter 3) is the first thing I look for.** You can rest stemming between two holds. You can stem between a wide variety of holds including smearing. The more flexible you

are, the wider you can stem...the more you can take advantage of widely separated holds. You can often stem without using your hands.

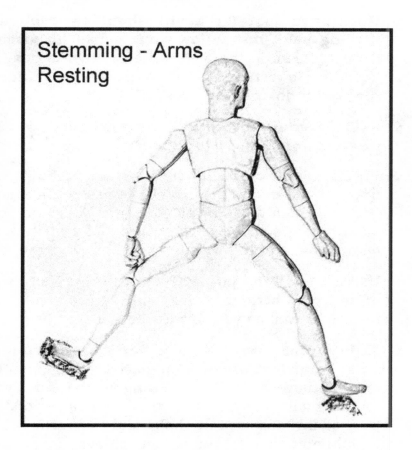

Stemming - Arms Resting

❖ **Hanging *straight-armed* on one or two arms.** Because your arm is straight, you are using your skeleton to hold the weight, rather than your arm muscles. It is best if the hand is high because you are closer to the cliff....and more of your weight is on your feet. If the cliff is somewhat overhung, hanging by one arm may not be effective because the benefit you gain to the resting arm may be offset by how much more your other arm tires...and switching from arm to arm gains nothing. If there isn't a high hold to hang from, you can sometimes kneel down in order to hang from your straight arm.

❖ **Hooking a foot (at about shoulder level) and leaning back may allow you to use no arms.** I saw a person do this with a knee bar in a box-like opening. He rested as he hung upside down under a roof...with no arms.

❖ **Resting your fingers and arms by placing your forearms on a chest-high ledge.**

❖ **Pushing your chin down on a ledge to hold your body in place.** You don't generate much force using your chin, but it can be all you need. This technique is seldom used. However, it does show how far climbers will go to meet the needs of the climb.

❖ **Using a good fist jam will allow you to hang with your arms straight**....allowing you to rest your fingers as well as your arms.

❖ **Maintaining yourself in a vertical position by using your feet under a ledge.** You wedge them in and cantilever your feet (by lifting the toe end of your foot up against the rock) so that your upper body is pushed into the rock...to help hold you vertical. You should note that: (1) you do not achieve a lot of force, but it may be enough to keep you from peeling away from the cliff, and (2) you do not want to fall back with your feet wedged into a crack. *If there is any chance that this could happen, don't use this technique, it could be extremely dangerous.*

❖ **Stuffing and wedging a knee, a shoulder, or even your whole body into an opening** can provide a rest.

Misuse of Figure 8 to Belay

The number one dangerous practice I have observed is where a figure 8 device is used as a belay device and the rope is threaded through the figure 8 as is done for rappelling. For severe leader falls, this approach is not adequate because it relies on friction, it does not "lock" like a standard belay device...and may be fatal for the leader.

An example of a severe fall occurs when a leader has climbed above a belay, has 10 feet of rope out, and falls 20 feet. This can generate a force equal to about 10 times the weight of the climber. If you are braking with a figure 8 threaded the way you rappel, and your leader takes a severe fall, you may lose skin from your hand...and the leader may die.

The really dangerous part of using a figure 8 in this manner is that for most belaying situations it will work. This generates a false sense of security. *It is much better to make a practice of using techniques that are safe for all situations.* Why develop a habit that, in some situations, could cause a fatality.

Swapping Hands and Feet

On occasion, you may find yourself using a hold but wishing you were using your other hand. Similarly, you may find you are on the wrong foot for what you want to do next. If the handhold or foothold is large enough, it is usually easy to swap from one foot (or hand) to the other. Listed below are a variety of ways to swap a foot or a hand when the hold is smaller:

❖ **Hop off the foot you are standing on and quickly replace it with the other foot.**

❖ **Cross your foot behind the foot you are standing on.**

❖ **Slide your foot down the inside of the leg you are standing on.** This allows you to more accurately place the inside of your foot on the hold...as you slide the other foot off.

❖ **Place your hand on top of the hand that is gripping the hold for small hand/finger swap.** Then replace one finger at a time...until the second hand is on the hold.

❖ **Change feet using momentum and smearing.** The following describes the steps used to move your left foot off a hold and replace it with your right foot:

1. Swing your body toward the right while at the same time smearing your right foot on the right wall face and *push.* (Your momentum will allow you to take your weight on this foot. These actions will stop your swing to the right....and start you swinging to the left.)

2. With your weight on your right foot, you can now take your left foot off the hold...and quickly smear it on the left wall face. (By now you are swinging to the left.)

3. As you swing to the left and your left foot is smeared on the wall, you can now push on your left foot (taking the weight off your right foot) and quickly, but carefully, place your right foot on the hold.

1, 2, and 3....You have now changed feet on the hold in one to two seconds.

❖ **You can simulate this action** by placing a dime on the floor. Place your left foot on the dime and your right foot about 18 inches to the right of the dime. Swing your upper body to the right until you have enough weight on your right foot to pick up your left foot....and then place it on the floor about 18 inches to the left of the dime. This will have started you swinging to the left...continue swinging left until you can move all your body weight onto your left foot. Pick up your right foot and place it on the dime. You have now swapped feet on the dime. This is easily done because the wall your feet are on is horizontal. However, in the rock climbing situation, your feet are pressed into a vertical wall and you have a lot of weight on your arms. Although the rock climbing situation is more strenuous because of the pull on your arms, the overall movement is the same. After doing it once on the rock, it becomes rather easy. Please note, you have to pay particular close attention to placing your foot rapidly and accurately on the hold.

Chapter 9

Mantles and Roofs

Mantles. Climbers frequently use mantles. It is a common move, one that many of us have used when we were young to climb over a high fence. The move consists of:

❖ Pulling your body up using both arms (commonly called a "pull-up")...usually done without help from your legs.

❖ Continuing this movement until your shoulders are at the level of your hands. I call this the "Semi-Mantle" position.

❖ Continuing further up until your arms are straight down with your weight pushing down on your arms. You are now in a full mantle.

❖ Exiting from the mantle position

Mantling. Mantles can be done using a ledge, handholds, and low angle smears. Mantles can also be done in a combination that uses one arm on a side pull and the other arm for a mantle.

When mantling, your hand and fingers may have to be adjusted. As you move up, if your fingers are wrapped over a small ledge, your hand flattens out and hangs off the ledge unless you adjust your hand. When your hand is flat and the weight is on your fingers, leverage is working against you. This results in excessive force on your fingers. This can be avoided by moving your palms onto the ledge to take your body weight as you move up.

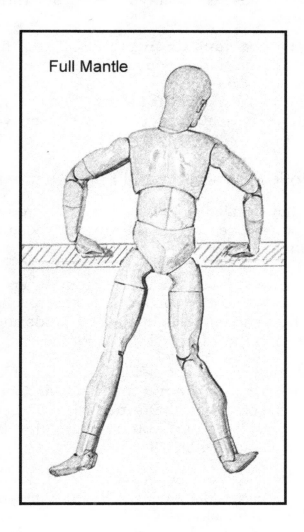

Full Mantle

You can begin to adjust your hands on the ledge when your shoulders reach the level of your hands. As you continue upward, start turning your elbows outward while turning your hands inward. This will let your palms (or, on small ledges, the outside of your palms) take your body weight off your fingers.

In addition, as you move up and your wrist bends backward, you lose the ability to have your thumb assist your fingers.

Mantling can be done on fingertips. If your fingers are very strong in relation to your weight, it may be possible to continue the mantle by going up on your fingertips rather than by turning your hands. This is very difficult to do, but it does allow you to mantle on very small edges.

Moves Following Mantle and Semi-Mantle Position

After you have pulled up with two hands, you now have to find a way to exit from the mantle position. Some considerations:

❖ The easiest thing that can occur when you do a mantle is find a foothold that is now reachable. This foothold can take weight off your hands and possibly free up an arm to reach for a hold.

❖ You may find a foothold that you can use as a highstep to exit from a mantle. This foothold may require some push/pull to move your body weight over your foot and you can use the techniques described in Chapter 3.

❖ You can also exit when you are in a semi-mantle position (shoulders at hand level) before you reach a full mantle position.

If you are strong enough, you can "lock-off" one arm. When you do this, you don't try to lift your body up, you just try to lock it in place so it doesn't fall. This will allow you to reach up with the other arm.

If you are not strong enough to lock your arm in place, you may be able to use a *rapid* sequence of:

➤ Using two arms to pull your shoulders quickly one to two inches above the ledge edge.

➤ "Locking-off" one arm as much as possible. It can help to have your shoulder pushed in as close as you can to your hand...and the cliff.

➤ Reaching for a hold with the other arm as fast as possible. As you reach for a hold, your body may slip down a little, but you still may have enough time to make the grab.

❖ You can exit a mantle by centering your weight over one hand, balancing on it, and lifting your other hand up for a hold. Stability can be improved if you keep your feet wide apart to keep your body from inadvertently twisting.

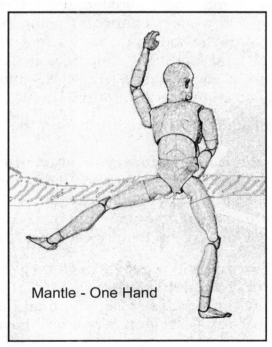

Mantle - One Hand

❖ One particular method of exiting from a mantle is used a lot, that is, placing one foot up on the same edge that your hands are on. This move can require a fair amount of flexibility and a fair amount of effort to get your body weight over your feet. In addition to the usual ways to move your body weight over your foot, you may be able to use the mantle itself to push you up. This can include going up on your finger tips.

Roof Considerations

Roofs, in particular, can be intimidating for novice climbers. However, *the novice climber should not be intimidated by roofs that are rated "easy."* There are roofs that are intimidating...and should be intimidating. However, these roofs are rated at a higher level of difficulty.

If the novice climber has been climbing at the 5.5 or 5.6 level, and the climb under consideration is rated at that level, he/she has a good chance of going through that particular roof. If the roof is an easier roof, there should be good hand- and footholds. This does not mean that it will be easy for a novice climber but it does mean he/she will have a good chance of going through it.

Things to consider when going through a roof:

❖ **Look for holds before you start up through a roof.** As was mentioned previously when going over a roof or bulge, you should pay particular attention to footholds that you may need but cannot see after you have moved up. Remember them!

❖ **Plan how you will move** through the roof. It may not be possible to plan your way all through the roof... you may not be able to see the final holds. This is okay, because a beginner roof will have hand and foot holds that a beginner requires to go through the roof. They should appear.

❖ **Be rested before going through the roof**. Going through a roof tends to be somewhat strenuous and frequently does not give you a place to rest once you have started.

❖ **Find a rest when going through a roof**. Although rests are not frequently found when going through a roof, consider the possibility that there might be a way to rest. It is better if you can observe a potential resting point before starting through the roof. However, it is possible to find a rest as you go through the roof, in particular, a stemming rest. On one particular double roof, I found that I could wedge my whole body in a small alcove for a rest after the first roof and (thankfully) before the second roof.

❖ **Keep as much weight on your feet as possible** when going through a roof. This is essential. This saves valuable arm strength. For this reason, you want to keep your feet on the rock, you do not want to let your feet swing away from the rock while you hang by your arms.

❖ **Look for a hold you can pull on.** The first thing I look for in going over a roof is a hold of some kind that will allow me to pull myself into the cliff. This hold can be an edge, a crack, etc. The hold that provides "pull" will allow you to push your feet either against a hold, or against the back wall where you can smear your feet. This keeps your feet on the rock and helps to save your arm strength.

❖ **Move without wasting any time.** When going through a roof, it will probably be strenuous from start to finish. This doesn't mean you shouldn't be thinking about the best moves or how to go, but it does mean that you should evaluate quickly and decisively...and go.

❖ **Look for a hold to push your feet against** when you are pulling with your hand(s), and you are near the roof edge. If this is a roof that isn't too deep, you may be able to use the wall that meets the underside of the roof...or you may find a hold on the underside of the roof. This foot push—arm pull can allow you to get a look over the edge. You need to see over the edge to identify holds that can be used to either pull yourself further up, or can be used by the foot. It is a good idea to do this even if your foot push-arm pull will only allow time for a short look.

If possible, the body should be pressed against the arm and be as close to the hand as possible. This reduces the leverage (and stress) on the arm. The other arm can then reach up for another hold.

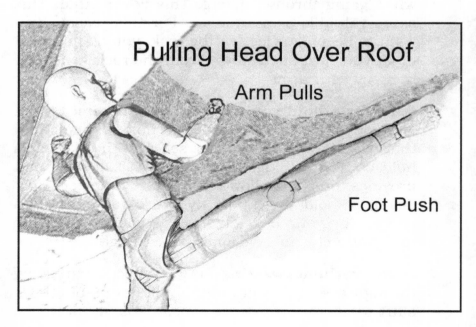

Pulling Head Over Roof

Arm Pulls

Foot Push

❖ Sometimes it is possible to wedge your foot in a crack on the face of the roof edge and use it as a step.... allowing you to pull up enough to go over the roof.

❖ Because each roof is unique, it must be evaluated by the climber just as is done when doing face or crack climbing. You can use the same combinations that are used in face climbing and crack climbing such as heel hooking, mantles, laybacks, etc.

Using Mantles to Keep from Peeling

You can also use the mantle position to keep from peeling away from the cliff. This is helpful even when you are using your feet to lift your body up. Typically, this occurs where there is a good hold to step on, and there is a ledge above it that can be used with your hands. The ledge provides downward pull, but not outward pull. If (while you are stepping on the foothold and lifting your body up) you leave weight on your hands as they move into a mantle position, you can generate friction to keep you from peeling. This friction will allow you to: (1) pull your waist-high hands (that are in a mantle position) in a direction away from the wall, and (2) force your shoulders into the cliff. You can continue to pull yourself into the cliff with one hand and reach for a hold with your other hand. It may help to lean your body slightly over the hand that remains on the ledge as you reach up with the other hand.

Chapter 10

Momentum and Dihedrals

Momentum is created by getting a mass, or weight, in motion. You can use momentum in climbing because a mass in motion tends to stay in motion (e.g., a ball stays in motion when thrown).

You use momentum in everyday life. For example, consider two methods that can be used to go up a set of stairs. You can: (1) step with a smooth weight transfer as you go from one step to the another, or (2) use momentum by springing up from stair to stair by stepping up with one foot and then throwing your center of gravity over this same foot by springing off your back leg. You can also use momentum by just jumping up the stairs. These are simple and common momentum moves, moves that we have all experienced. The question is, how can momentum be used as a climbing tool.

Momentum Moves—Requirements

❖ A way to generate the motion needed to create momentum ... such as a push from a foot.

❖ A way to complete the move, such as catching your balance, grabbing a hold that is now in reach, etc.

Using Momentum for Climbing

A few of the various ways to use momentum are outlined below:

❖ One simple use of momentum is to have a spring in your step when you move from hold to hold. This is the same approach as in the stairs example mentioned above. I find it is easier on my arms and my legs if I spring somewhat when moving from hold to hold. However, when you are in a delicate balance situation, it may be better to use slow, smooth, and non-dynamic moves.

❖ Frequently, you will find that you can step up quickly and the resultant momentum will give you time to grab a hold before you peel away from the cliff. This is fairly obvious from the beginning.

❖ Sometimes you are in a position where your weight is primarily on your feet and both hands must be kept on holds to keep you from peeling (or barndooring) from the cliff. In addition, you would like to use an arm to reach up for a hold, but in this situation you cannot because you would peel away. Frequently, you can get around this situation by using momentum as follows. First, get in position by leaning the upper body slightly away from the cliff with your head back and leave your waist close to the cliff. Second, in rapid sequence, take the following actions:

➢ Using your arms, pull and throw your upper body and head toward the cliff (the stomach muscles may provide some assistance) bending at the waist as you do so. This will throw your chest and head toward the cliff.

➢ As your upper body is thrown and moving toward the cliff, reach up for, and grab, the hold, you want. This should be done as quickly as possible...immediately after you have created the momentum generated by throwing your upper body at the cliff.

This move does not generate a lot of momentum but it does take a little time for your body to move toward the cliff, slow down, stop, and start to move away from the cliff. While this is taking place, it can provide enough time to make a grab for a hold.

I use this technique frequently. It can be used for situations involving two regular handholds, and for situations where you are using a semi-mantle hold to keep from peeling.

❖ Sometimes when your hands are taking a lot of your body weight (e.g., when your feet are smearing), it is not possible to use the momentum move as described in the previous situation to reach up for a hold. However, it may be possible to free up an arm to make a grab for a hold by using a variation of the technique described in Chapter 8 for changing feet as follows:

  ➢ If you want to reach up with your right hand, swing your hips to the left weighting your left foot as you do so.

  ➢ As your weight shifts to the left foot, step harder on the foot and reach up with your right hand for the hold.

This sideways momentum will keep you from barndooring as you let go of your right hand. If you are having trouble visualizing this description, go back and review the "dime" simulation movement described in Swapping Feet in Chapter 8. It is very close to the same set of movements...In both cases you are using a sideways momentum to take the weight off a foot so that you can move it.

❖ Similarly, when you are in the above situation but the hold is still slightly out of reach, you can use another variation to both lift your body up a short distance and free up a hand for the grab. Assuming you want to reach up with your left hand, this can be accomplished by:

➤ Swinging your hips to the right weighting your right foot as you do so.

➤ As your weight shifts to the right, press your right foot to the wall and take your body weight on that foot. This will unweight the left foot.

➤ Move your left foot higher up and smear it on the wall and press your right foot harder. This will start your body swinging to the left.

➤ Take your body weight on that foot as your body swings to the left.

➤ With your weight on the left foot, simultaneously step up on the left foot and pull up on the right arm (lifting your body up somewhat), and immediately reach up with your left hand to make the grab for the hold.

I wouldn't call this an easy move, it does take practice and it happens fairly quickly. Knowing how high you can safely move your foot up and getting the timing right can be tricky.

❖ Sideways momentum, as described above, can be used in other situations. It can be used to readjust your foot when doing a layback, a stem etc. Experiment.

❖ Moving your center of gravity over your bent foot to get your body in position for a highstep can sometimes be accomplished using momentum. This was briefly mentioned in Chapter 3. If you hear someone tell you to "rock on over your foot," they are telling you to use momentum to lunge in a way that will move your center of gravity over your leg, the one that will be doing the highstep. The leg that you are going to do the highstep on, must be somewhat close to your body and, depending on your flexibility, can be almost as high as your waist.

❖ Throwing your body up so that both arms and feet are not touching the rock is the ultimate momentum move. A move like this is called a dynamic move, or a "dyno." It can be accomplished by throwing yourself up by feet alone, both hands and feet, just arms (for those who are extremely strong), and one arm (for those who are super human).

Dihedrals

Dihedrals are where two vertical rock wall faces come together at approximately a 90 degree angle. In other words, it looks like the corner of a room where two walls meet.

Dihedrals can be particularly easy when there are numerous footholds. Even very small footholds are easier to use on a dihedral than on a wall because you are typically stemming between the walls. This stemming automatically forces your foot into the wall thereby improving the use of a small hold. In addition, frequently a crack can be found, and used, where the two walls meet. If there is no foothold on one side, you can smear on one side while creating the force necessary to smear by: (1) using your other foothold to push on the opposite wall while in a stemming position, (2) using your hands to layback on a hold, or the crack between the two walls, and (3) etc.

Dihedrals can be more difficult when the walls have no apparent holds and they are smooth. These dihedrals can be climbed using the crack found at the intersection of the two walls utilizing the following steps:

❖ From the ground find a hold in the crack that you can pull on with your right hand. You want a hold you can pull toward you and somewhat to the left. It is best if the height of the hold is about midway between head high, and as high as you can reach.

❖ Face the corner and smear your right foot on the wall about knee high.

❖ Smear your left hand on the wall about waist high or slightly lower. Your fingers should be pointing downward at approximately an 8 o'clock position.

❖ Now you will use your right foot, right arm, and left arm to lift your left foot on the wall into a smearing position. The left foot should be targeted to go about as high, or slightly higher than, your right foot. You lift your left foot by pushing down with your left arm while at the same time pulling on your right arm and pushing with your right foot.

It may be difficult to visualize this move. However, in practice it is really not difficult. To better understand this move you can simulate it at home. Go to a set of stairs and place your right foot on the third stair at the corner where the stair meets the right wall. Then grab high up on the right handrail with your right hand. Then bend down and place your left hand on the fourth stair (about two feet to the left of the right wall) and push down. You should find that you can easily pick your left foot up and place it where you want. This simulation is very close to the same move as is done on the rock.

❖ You now are off the ground with your feet smeared on the walls. You continue by lifting your body up somewhat and use your left hand to find a hold in the crack above your right hand, a hold that you can pull on (toward you and somewhat to the right).

❖ You then take your right hand from the crack and smear it on the right wall down near your waist in the same manner that you did using the left hand.

❖ You then lift your right leg using the same technique described to lift your left leg. This time you push down with your right hand, pull the crack with your left hand, and push your left leg into the wall. You can now lift your right leg and smear it higher on the wall.

❖ You can repeat these steps going back and forth until you are at the top of the dihedral.

Dihedrals can be even more challenging if there are sections of the crack that are difficult to use.

I find there is a tendency to stay in a stem position as I climb, however, there are occasions when it is best to leave the stem and face climb on one of the faces.

In addition, to the extent a hold or even a rough texture on a wall is available, try to take advantage of the situation. If you have been using smearing holds and a regular hold suddenly appears, it may be helpful to use as a rest.

Sometimes using a regular hold to step on will reduce the force on the opposing smeared foot to your disadvantage.

You may find it better to use the hold in a way that will create the opposing force necessary to keep your other foot smeared on.

Moving Foot under Body Weight

Another method of getting your center of gravity over a foot is to move the foot, rather than your body, as is more commonly done. This can be accomplished even if your knee is bent and your leg weighted. You may be able to hop and slide one foot toward and under your body. Not easy, but possible in some situations.

Chapter 11

Summary / Conclusion

- ❖ **Receive proper training from a professional licensed guide before you actually climb.**

- ❖ **Search diligently for holds** that you can use. Spend as much time looking down for footholds as you do looking up for handholds. Make sure to look for side pulls and holds under bulges. Look for the best part of the crack, handhold, etc., to use.

- ❖ **Adjust your hand and fingers as you grip a handhold** to maximize effectiveness. Try to get your thumb involved in some manner.

- ❖ **Observe how other climbers use their feet, hands, fingers, and body position.** What part of the shoe do they use? How do they place, or smear, their foot on a hold? Do they use their thumb? How do they use it? How close is their body to the cliff? How are they pulling, and how are they pushing? Do they move slowly in balance, or do they move with momentum?

- ❖ **Keep your arms and fingers rested when you can.** Enter a difficult section rested. Hang straight armed to conserve strength. When you need a rest, look for a place you can stem. Do not move a hand or foot off a hold until you know where it is going.

❖ **Evaluate your options and plan as much as you can** when approaching a difficult, strenuous section such as a roof. Take the time to select good holds and make good moves as you go, but **do not waste time.**

❖ **Experiment with different body positions.** How do the forces on your arms and legs change as you move your body from one position to another? Is there a way to do a mantle? A highstep?

Go climb...and have fun.

Appendix I—The Climbing Process

This appendix is written for those who have never climbed and do not understand the process used by a leader and a follower. It briefly touches on the process of top roping.

The process of getting up the cliff normally requires that you have a leader and a follower. There are other ways to get up the cliff: (1) climbing alone without using a rope for safety, and (2) climbing alone and using a special technique and equipment to protect you. This writeup will cover the usual method that uses a leader and a follower.

The write-up will not cover the specifics of how the leader and the follower use gear. As previously mentioned, and it is worth repeating, gear use and safety techniques should be learned in person, and **you should be certain that you learn from a person who not only understands climber safety, but is also someone who can train and pass on this required safety information to you.**

This writeup, however, will introduce the basic climbing terms and it will describe the climbing process. This should give the reader who has not climbed a picture of the steps required to ascend the cliff.

Follower and Leader—The Process

To climb the cliff, we will have a leader and a follower. Novice climbers are followers. In this description, let's assume that you are the follower and I am the leader. To reach the top of the cliff, we take the following steps:

1. **We both tie into the rope.** I tie into one end and you tie into the other end.

2. **You insert the rope in your belay locking device** that is appropriately connected to your harness.

   Note: A belay locking device allows you to feed the rope through it (allowing the other person to climb) and at any time it can also be used to "lock off" the rope (allowing you to catch a person who falls). To "Belay" (used as a verb) refers to a person using a belay device.

3. **I ask** "On Belay?"

4. **You say "Belay on, climb when ready."** This lets me know you are in position to feed the rope as needed, and that you are prepared to lock off and catch me.

5. **I answer** "Climbing"...You respond "Climb On."

6. **I start to climb the cliff** as you feed the rope through your belay device.

7. **I reach up** and insert a piece of protection in the cliff.

   This example assumes you are doing traditional climbing or "trad" climbing. Trad climbing means that protection (e.g., a "nut" or a device that cams) is placed by the climber into a crack in a way that will stay stuck should the leader fall. Another form of climbing is called "sport climbing."

   In sport climbing the protection (usually a bolt embedded in the wall) is permanently fixed in the wall. This means the leader doesn't have to insert the protection, he/she can just clip into it.

8. **I clip the rope into the protection.** This means that the rope is now running from your belay device

up through the protection (that I just placed) and from there to my waist

9. **I continue to climb and continue to add, and clip into, more pieces of protection.** If I fall part way up, you "lock off" the rope with your belay device and catch me. Note that when I am above my protection, I will fall twice as far as the distance from my waist to the protection...plus the slack in the rope...plus any stretch in the rope

10. **I stop and set up an anchoring system** when I have used up most of the rope and have found an area to set up a "belay." The term belay (used as a noun) refers to a section of the climb that has an anchor system that will give the climbers a safe place to tie into, a place where they can meet and exchange gear. The leader inserts protection into the rock and ties the gear together to create a single integrated system of protection...with appropriate redundancies built in.Note, when belay is referred to as a noun, it is the place where the leader stops to set up an anchoring system for the climbers to meet and exchange gear. It should not be confused with belay used as a verb. As mentioned in step 2, "to belay" refers to a climber protecting another climber utilizing a belay device.

11. **I tie myself into the anchoring system.**

12. **I call to you "Belay Off"** telling you I am tied into an anchor system and do not need your belay protection.

13. **You yell back "Off Belay"** when you have removed the rope from your belay device (letting me know the rope is ready to be pulled up).

It is very important to have good communication

between the follower and the leader. Sometimes you can be in a situation where it is difficult to hear each other (e.g., because you are 150 feet apart and the follower is under a large roof). In these situations, sometimes climbers use an agreed-to system of signals (using "rope tugs") as a means of communication.

14. **I pull up the rope** until it pulls on you and **you yell "That's me."**

15. **I place the rope in my belay device, pull up any slack rope, and yell "Belay on"** letting you know that you can climb because I am ready to protect you if you fall.

16. **You yell "Climbing"** when you are ready to climb. **I answer "Climb on"** letting you know I realize you are about to start climbing and am ready to belay you.

17. **You climb up the cliff.** I pull the rope through my belay device as you climb.

18. **You remove the protection** that I inserted in the cliff...as you climb.

    Your nut tool is used to help you remove protection when it is stuck in the cliff.

If you fall while climbing, I brake the rope using my belay device and catch you. With the rope above, you will only fall as far as the slack in the rope and any stretch in the rope...very little.

19. **When you reach me at the belay, you tie into the belay.**

20. **You give me the gear** that you collected as you climbed. This completes one full "pitch" of climbing.

We are back where we started at the bottom, I have the gear I need to start leading again and you are ready to belay me for the next pitch.

21. **You insert the rope in your belay.**

22. **You tell me "On Belay," I say "Climbing" and you say "Climb on"** ....and we start the second pitch... Now we repeat the steps we used to climb from the ground. This continues on until we reach the top.

The execution of the steps can differ between trad climbing and sport climbing, but the overall climbing process as described is the same.

Top Roping—The Process

Top rope climbing refers to using an anchor system similar to, but not the same as, a belay setup. One of the climbers finds a way to get up the cliff, e.g., hiking up the backside of the cliff and sets up an anchor. A rope is then appropriately threaded through the anchor and both ends of the rope are dropped to the ground. The steps to use are:

1. **The climbing partner ties into one end of the rope.**

2. **The belaying partner pulls on the other end of the rope to remove the slack**...and is slightly pulling on the climber.

3. **The belaying partner inserts the rope in his/her belay device.** The rope is now running from the belay device up through the top rope anchor system and back down to the climber.

4. **The climber asks "On Belay?"** and when the

belayer is prepared to go, responds **"Belay on climb when ready."**

5. **The climber calls out "Climbing" and the belayer when ready calls out "Climb on."**

6. **The climber climbs. The belayer pulls the rope down through his/her belay device** to keep the slack out of the rope as the climber goes up. The belayer is ready to lock off the belay device should the climber fall.

7. **The climber notifies the belayer he/she is ready to come down** when he/she has reached the top.

8. **The climber comes down.** The climber has a choice of being lowered by the belayer, or by rappelling down. Whichever choice is made, it is extremely important that both the belayer and the climber know what the climber intends to do.

   The climber may say **"Lower me when ready"** and the belayer can respond **"Ready to lower you."** The belayer can then allow the rope to slide at a speed acceptable to the climber as he/she is lowered to the ground.

   The climber may decide to rappel down. If so, the climber should safely tie into the anchor system. He/she can then yell down **"Off belay."** The belayer can then take the rope out of his/her belay device and yell back **"Belay is off."** The climber should then properly place the ropes in a rappel device... and rappel down to the ground.

   Before the belayer takes the climber off belay, he/she should be absolutely certain that the person is tied in and intends to rappel.

Appendix II—A Few Thoughts for the New Leader

To be a safe lead climber you need two thing: (1) the technical skills necessary for leading, and (2) the mental skills that provide the confidence and good judgment necessary to lead. The mental skills are not always obvious. The following situations explore this area a bit:

❖ **A leader is exposed to taking a longer fall than a follower.** When you are a follower, the rope is usually directly over you and if you fall, it will be a very short one. However, when you are a leader you are above the rope. The length of the fall is a function of the distance the leader is above the protection that catches him/her. Depending upon the frequency of placing gear, this can be a long fall. This can cause a leader to be apprehensive. Suddenly, you think a piece of protection looks like it might have a chance of falling out. This becomes a mental game. This can place stress on the leader. However, it is also part of the challenge of leading. Some climbers never decide to lead...others want to lead most of the time. Leading takes technical skill, good judgment, and the ability to stay calm in a difficult situation.

❖ **Worst Fall Was Off Route**. When you begin to lead, it is very important that you stay on route. If you inadvertently go off route you may end up trying to climb a 5.10 when you thought you were doing a 5.6. Worse, the ability to place protection may be extremely difficult and dangerous. If you are leading a 5.6, and the moves are much tougher than that, or the protection is supposed to be easy and you can't find anywhere to place protection, **You are more than likely off route!** Stop before you commit yourself into a dangerous situation.

❖ **Protect your follower on a traverse.** A leader should place protection on a traverse that will minimize the risk of a fall by the follower. Consider a 20 foot traverse with the crux move in the middle of the traverse. The best place *for the leader* to protect himself/herself is just before the crux. This way if he/she slips and falls, the gear is right next to him/her and the resultant fall is short. However, when the follower traverses and removes this same gear, he/she is now faced with going through this same crux move. If the leader did not place protection for some distance after the crux (the climbing may have been easy after the crux, and the leader felt safe without inserting any more protection), the follower could be facing a long serious fall. The leader should protect a follower by placing protection on a traverse more frequently and soon after a difficult move.

❖ **Choice of gear or grip.** Sometimes the hold you want is the same place you would like to place gear, and there isn't room for both gear and a handhold. You have to make a decision, should I place gear for protection or should I forego the gear protection and use the handhold? There is no single answer to the question. However, you should consider:

➤ The consequences of a fall if you don't place the gear. What is the potential bodily harm if you fall? If you have another good piece placed a couple feet below, the answer may be that there is little risk. If the potential fall is very long overlooking some ugly looking rocks sticking out below you, the best decision is probably to place the gear.

> ➤ How sure are you that you can make the move if you don't place the gear?

> ➤ If you make the move what is the difficulty of the moves that immediately follow?

> ➤ If you make the move, how soon will you be able to place protection and what is the difficulty of placing this protection?

Sometimes this decision can be made even more difficult because you are in a strenuous position. You cannot waste a lot of time deciding because your arms are getting tired as you evaluate and decide. It might be good to think about this type of situation before it occurs so that you can make a good, and quick decision, when you need to.

❖ **Rope Drag**. When placing protection a leader should be aware of the potential for rope drag. Rope drag is the result of protection being placed back and forth in a zigzag manner up the cliff. That is, the rope goes left and right, back and forth up the cliff. Sometimes a climber is forced to zigzag by virtue of the route's path. This can result in 50 or more pounds of pull on the leader. Not something you want to have when you are moving up an easy section, let alone a difficult section. Every leader I know has been caught by rope drag at one time or another. You do not forget the experience. When you see a potential for creating rope drag, try placing gear in a way that will minimize sharp zigzagging turns.

❖ **Sport Climbing vs. Trad Climbing.** A few leader considerations regarding the differences between sport and trad climbing:

> ➤ Route finding is not a major issue in sport climbing...just follow the fixed protection.

> ➤ Rope drag is not generally an issue in sport climbing. The fixed protection typically does not zigzag.

> ➤ Trad protection has a chance of being dislodged and falling out. Proper sport climbing protection has very little chance of failing.

> ➤ A rope can be clipped to protection rather easily with sport climbing. A quickdraw, or a sling with two carabiners, is clipped to the anchor and the rope. Trad climbing requires taking the *additional steps* of: (1)selecting the best place to insert protection, (2) selecting a piece of protection that will fit (sometimes this has to be done more than once), and (3) inserting and testing the protection.

Based on these differences, a climber may be more willing to push his/her limits more on sport climbing.

Appendix III—Analysis of Climbing Forces

The objective of this section is to increase your understanding of climbing forces. Knowing how to quantify climbing forces will not make you a better climber, however, the following writeup may improve your understanding of the magnitude of: (1) the forces involved in climbing, and (2) the changes that occur in these forces as you reposition your body.

Climbing forces can be computed in the same way a bridge is analyzed. This analysis will assume: (1) the climber weighs 150 pounds, and (2) the climber's center of gravity is located at the hips. This is probably a little off, but the assumption should be close enough to reasonably demonstrate the magnitude of several climbing forces.

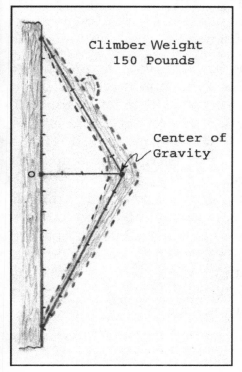

Climber Weight
150 Pounds

Center of
Gravity

The opposing figure shows a climber outlined in dashed lines. It also shows the lines of force as they flow through the climber. The climber is pushing on his/her feet and pulling on the arms. The following write-up and the associated diagrams will compute the forces on the climber in three situations: (1) climber close to the wall, (2) climber far from the wall, and (3) the initial position with the climber midway between these two positions.

Since the forces are proportional to the length

of the line that represent these forces, we can calculate the forces by measuring the length of the lines. Close enough for our purposes.

Climber—Initial Position

This analysis assumes the climber is in a static position with no movement. Therefore, the sum of the horizontal and the vertical forces on the center of gravity is zero.

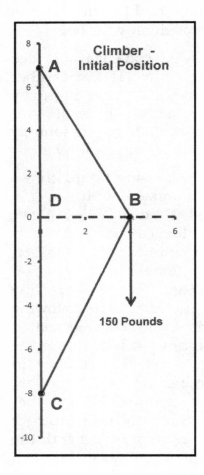

Every force can be broken down into a horizontal component and a vertical component. In the diagram the arm pulls the center of gravity from point B toward point A. This force has a horizontal component (from point B to point D) and a vertical component (a line from point B directly upward, one as long as it is from point D to point A).

The opposing figure shows a figure with 150 pounds pulling down at the waist. Given that this is a static situation, there are also 150 pounds pushing upward. This is the upward vertical component force of the arms and the legs. The vertical arm force is line D to A (7 units) and the vertical leg force is C to D (8 units)...total 15 units long. Thus, the 150 pounds of upward force is represented by 15 units of length...or 10 pounds per unit of length.

The horizontal arm pull is B to D, 4 units long or 40 pounds (4 times 10 #/unit) pulling the waist toward the cliff.

The horizontal foot push is equal to, and in the opposite direction of, this horizontal arm pull (the sum of the horizontal forces on point B must equal zero). Therefore, the force of the foot into the wall must also be 4 units or 40 pounds.

The arms and body are 8 units long and are pulling a total 80 pounds (8 times 10 #/unit), and the feet are 9 units long and are pushing a total 90 pounds (9 units times 10 #/unit).

Climber—Near

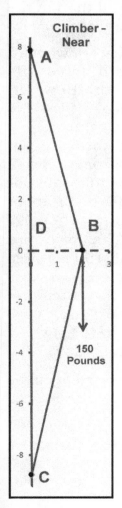

The Climber—Near figure shows the climber closer to the wall than shown in the initial figure.

The vertical downward and upward force still sum to zero. However, when we look at the two vertical components, they now measure for arm pull (from A to D) about 7.75 units, and for leg push (D to C) about 8.75 units for a total of 16.5 units. The downward force is still 150 pounds, and therefore, in this situation, the force per unit is 9.1 pounds per unit (150 pounds divided by 16.5 units pushing upward).

Note that the force per unit of length has changed as the length of the vertical component has gotten longer.

The horizontal component of arm pull is 2 units or 18.2 pounds (2 times 9.1 #/unit). Likewise, the horizontal push into the cliff is 18.2 pounds.

Again, to complete the picture, the arms are pulling 72.8 pounds (8 units times 9.1 #/unit), and the feet are pushing 81.9 pounds (9 units times 9.1 #/unit).

In summary, the horizontal force holding your foot on a hold has dropped from 40 pounds to 18.2 pounds...a dramatic reduction resulting from being closer to the cliff. Also, the force on the arms has dropped from 80 pounds to 72.8 pounds and the force on the legs has dropped from 90 pounds to 81.9 pounds.

Climber—Far

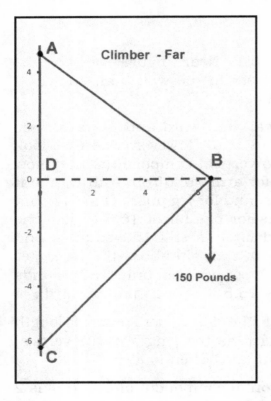

The Climber -Far figure shows the climber further from the wall than in the initial figure.

The vertical downward and upward force still sums up to zero. However, when we look at the two vertical components, they now measure for arm pull (from A to D) about 4.75 units, and for leg push (D to C) about 6.25 units for a total of 11 units. The downward force is still 150 pounds, and therefore, in this situation the force per unit is 13.6 #/unit (150 pounds divided by 11 units pushing upward).

Note that the force per unit of length has changed again as the length of the vertical component has gotten shorter.

The horizontal component of arm pull is 6.5 units or 88.4 pounds (6.5 times 13.6 #/unit). Likewise, the horizontal push into the cliff is 88.4 pounds.

Again, to complete the picture, the arms are pulling 108.8 pounds (8 units times 13.6 #/unit), and the feet are pushing 122.4 pounds (9 units times 13.6 #/unit).

In summary, the horizontal force holding your foot on a hold has increased from the initial 40 pounds to 88.4 pounds...an increase resulting from being further from the cliff. However, the force on the arms has increased from the initial 80 pounds to 108.8 pounds and the force on the legs has increased from 90 pounds to 122.4 pounds.

Climber Force —Summary

❖ Forces can change dramatically as you adjust your body position. In our example, the horizontal force pushing the foot onto a hold ranged from 18.2 pounds to 88.4 pounds.

❖ The further your waist is from the cliff, and the closer your hands are to your feet, the more your feet push horizontally on a hold and the more force is required by your arms and feet. The example of a climber far from the cliff is typical of a layback position. Note in our example that both feet and arms had forces in excess of 100 pounds.

❖ The closer your waist is to the cliff, the more you move your weight away from your arms to your feet The offset to this is that there is less horizontal force pushing your feet into the cliff.

However, with a good foothold, you don't really need a horizontal push to keep your foot on the hold, so you can keep your body close to the cliff to take as much weight off your hands and arms as possible.

Note: When you move your arms and body up the cliff, you will be losing horizontal foot force. Sometimes it is better to gain some momentum when your foot has good horizontal force on it...and then use the momentum to go through the area where your foot might slip off.

Note that all these examples show the climber bending at the waist to reach out for a hold. If the climber keeps the body straight at the waist and reaches from the shoulder for the hold, he/she will be closer to the cliff. This will result in more weight on the feet, less on the arms, and less horizontal force on the feet into the wall.

Appendix IV—Glossary of Terms

Aid Climbing—The climber can pull on either the rope, or protection anchored to the rock, to climb. The climber is "aided" by the protection.

Anchor—Protection set into the rock. The climber or the rope can be attached to the anchor. Natural protection such as a tree can also be used as an anchor.

Anchor system—Several pieces of gear set into the rock tied together into a single integrated unit. This should have redundancy built into the system. The system should not depend on any single piece of protection or any single sling.

Arête—Rock that sticks out in a narrow edge similar to the way a nose protrudes from the face.

Arm Bar—An arm placed in a crack where the hand pushes against one side of the crack's inner face and the elbow or upper arm pushes against the other inner face.

Barndooring—A climber swinging out away from the rock face when using one foothold and one handhold. The climber swings out from these two holds like a "swinging barn door." See Chapter 5 for more information.

Belay Device—Device used to protect another climber. As rope is threaded through the device allowing the other climber to move, it can be locked off to keep the rope from moving. See Climbing Gear figure in Chapter 2.

Belay (noun)—A place where a leader has set up an anchor system at the end of a pitch of climbing. The belay is used as a place for the follower to meet, and transfer the gear he has collected to the leader.

Belay (verb)—the act of protecting a climber utilizing a belay device.

Beta—Information or suggestions that will help a person climb. Note, do not provide unless a climber has stated that he/she would like this assistance.

Bolt—Bolts inserted and permanently fixed in the wall for use as an anchor.

Bouldering—Climbing near the ground without the use of a rope for protection. Frequently done with large pads placed below the climber for safety.

Cam—A mechanical piece of protection with a trigger that can be pulled to change the width of the protection. This allows it to fit various size cracks. A spring forces the protection against the two opposing side walls. They are also called **"friends."** See Climbing Gear figure in Chapter 2.

Carabiner—An oval shaped metal ring with a spring loaded gate. This is used for connecting rope to anchors, climbers to anchors, a nut tool to your harness, etc. See Climbing Gear figure in Chapter 2.

Climb Ratings—Climbs are rated for difficulty of climbing and difficulty of placing protection. The best climbs are also rated for quality using a star rating. See Chapter 2 for more information.

Crag—A small cliff/climbing area.

Crux—The most difficult section of the climb. This is the move that determines the level of difficulty of the climb.

Dihedral—The intersection of two vertical wall planes, typically at 90 degrees (approximately). It looks similar to two walls meeting in the corner of a room.

Dyno—This is a climber's dynamic move where the climber

throws his/her body in a manner that the arms, feet, and body lose contact with the rock.

Face Climbing—Climbing that uses few, or no, friction or crack holds.

Figure 8 (Gear)—Metal 8-shaped piece designed for use as a rappel device.

Figure 8 Knot—Knot most commonly used to tie the rope into the harness.

Finger Jam—Finger hold used in a narrow crack. See Chapter 7 for more information.

Fist Jam—Use of a fist as a hold in a two to three inch crack. See Chapter 7 for more information.

Flagging—Use of the unweighted foot to keep your body from turning inappropriately by lightly touching the foot against the wall. See Chapter 5 for more information.

Flake—A piece of stone that looks like it is peeling, or "flaking" away from the rock face. See Chapter 6 for more information.

Follower—The climber following the leader on a climb. See Appendix I—The Climbing Process for details.

Foot Jam—Wedging your foot, or feet, into a crack as a hold. See Chapter 7 for more information.

Free Climbing—Climbing without the use of ropes, etc., for protection. Also called **"climbing solo."**

Friction Climbing—Climbing that uses predominantly friction (smearing) holds. See Chapter 6 for more information.

Friend—A mechanical piece of protection with a trigger that can be pulled to change the width of the protection. This allows it to fit various size cracks. A spring forces the protection against the two opposing side walls. They are also called **"cams."** See Climbing Gear figure in Chapter 2.

Hand Jams—Use of a hand as a hold in a one to two inch crack. See Chapter 7 for more information.

Heel Hooking—Moving your leg up, and onto, a ledge or hold. Heel hooking helps to relieve the weight on your arms. See Chapter 6.

Highstep—Stepping up on a hold and lifting your body up as you are balanced over your foot...minimizing use of your arms. See Chapter 3 for detailed information.

Jug—The best possible handhold you can imagine; one that can be gripped, and pulled on, easily.

Knee Bar—Forcing a knee and foot against the two inner walls of a crack to create a hold. See Chapter 7 for more information.

Layback—Pulling on the arms and pushing on the feet to keep your body in place. See Chapter 5 for more information.

Leader—The person who: (1) climbs first by placing protection, and (2) builds an anchoring system to create a belay. See Appendix I, The Climbing Process for more information.

Mantle—Lifting your body up with your arms until your shoulders are above your hands and your arms are straight down. See Chapter 9 for more information.

Nut— A wire loop embedded in a wedge shaped piece of metal (usually aluminum). The metal piece is wedged in a crack in the rock and the metal loop is attached to a rope, or sling, using a carabiner.

Also called **"stoppers**." See Climbing Gear figure in Chapter 2.

Nut Tool—A thin metal tool used to remove nuts and other gear wedged into the rock for protection. See Climbing Gear figure in Chapter 2

Peeling—The upper part of your body falling away from the cliff because your center of gravity is further from the cliff than your feet, and you are not pulling your upper body toward the cliff.

Pinch Grip—Squeezing a hold between your thumb and fingers to create a hold. See Chapter 4 for more information.

Pitch—A section of climb that begins where the leader leaves the follower, and ends where the leader establishes a belay. See Appendix I, The Climbing Process for more information.

Piton— Spike-like metal piece driven into the rock with a hammer for use as protection.

Pocket—Indentation or hole in the rock that can be used as a hold.

Protection—An anchor in the rock, either one created by a climber inserting a piece of gear in the rock (e.g., a nut, a cam, etc.), or a natural anchor such as a tree. It also includes the slings, carabiners, etc., that work with the anchor to provide protection. See Climbing Gear figure in Chapter 2.

Prusiks—Two circular loops of climbing cord, one smaller than the other, used to ascend the rope. See Climbing Gear figure in Chapter 2.

Quick Draw—Short length of nylon webbing with a carabiner permanently fixed in either end. It is used primarily by a leader for attaching an anchor to the rope.

Ring Hold—Two fingers used with thumb to create a hold in a crack about an inch wide. See Chapter 7 for more information.

"Rock onto your foot"—Recommendation to give a sideways lunge that will move your body weight into a balanced position over your foot...so that you can do a highstep on that foot.

Roof—A wide section of rock that sticks out from the cliff... at least one to two feet.

Side Pull—A vertical edge or handhold that provides a horizontal pull (or push). It may, or may not, allow any downward pull. See Chapters 3 and 5 for more information.

Sling—A loop (24 inches is common, but they do vary in length) of nylon webbing. Also called a **"Runner."** See Climbing Gear figure in Chapter 2.

Smear—A friction hold using either a hand or a foot. See Chapter 6 for more information.

Sport Climbing—Climbing on protection permanently fixed in the rock...as opposed to trad climbing where the leader places protection in the rock and the follower retrieves it.

Stoppers—A wire loop embedded in a wedge shaped piece of metal (usually aluminum). The metal piece is wedged in a crack in the rock and the metal loop is attached to a rope, or sling, using a carabiner. Also called **"nuts."** See Climbing Gear figure in Chapter 2.

Top Rope (noun)—Anchor system built up high on the rock with a rope threaded through it with both ends of the rope on the ground. This system is used to protect climbers.

Top Roping (verb)—Climbing is done using a top rope anchor as protection. See Top Rope section in Appendix I, The Climbing Process.

Traditional (Trad) Climbing—Protection is placed in the rock by the leader and the follower retrieves it...as opposed to Sport Climbing, where protection is fixed permanently in the rock.

Traverse—A section of the climb that moves horizontal, rather than vertical.

Tri Cam—A passive cam, that is it is not spring loaded. The camming action is the result of the way it is placed in the rock. See Climbing Gear figure in Chapter 2. It can also be wedged like a nut with no camming.

Undercling—Gripping the rock with your hand/fingers in an upward position.

Yosemite Decimal System—The system used in the U.S. to rate climb difficulty. For more information, see Chapter 2.

About the Author

ROBERT BURBANK took up climbing at the age of 51. From that point on, he climbed as often as he could. He, and his wife Kathryn, live in upstate New York not too far from the Shawangunks. He has climbed from California to New Hampshire and partnered with climbers from many U. S. states, Canada, Europe, the Mid-East, and South America. His climbing culminated at the age of 57 when he climbed The Muir Wall route on El Capitan over a 6 day period...climbing 15 to 18 hours every day.

He has always been involved in sports. Prior to climbing, he ran 20 marathons including 10 New York's and 5 Boston's. Prior to that; tennis, skiing, hockey, etc.

His other pursuits include being an artist. At his most recent exhibit in Old San Juan, Puerto Rico, he was awarded a UNESCO medal by the French Consul for his Impressionism paintings. He also likes to play the ancient game of GO.

He has a bachelor's degree in engineering and a master's degree in business.

Books can be ordered from various online websites or by going to the authors website at www.elementsofclimbing. com. You can contact the author at this website.

Acknowledgments

Thanks to the people who trained and introduced me to climbing; R L and Karen Stolz of Alpine Adventures. I thank you for being such great instructors, and for making the experience so much fun.

Thanks to Sue Schiappa for all the editing you did. Editing text written by an engineer is not an easy task. Thanks again Sue.

Thanks to the hundreds of people that I partnered with over the years. With very few exceptions you were great.

Thanks to Frank Tkac, the best mountaineer and rock climber I know, for teaming up with me on one of my first climbs, and for teaming up with me later on our El Capitan climb...and for your dry wit.

Thanks to Bart Calkins for the many times we climbed together. You showed me how to select climbs, and avoid wasting time...allowing us to make an incredible number of climbs each day.

Thanks to Kim Ashley for all the times when we climbed together and for leading me up some of the best climbs I have ever done.

Thanks to my latest partner Lou Palumbo, for the many times we climbed and for being so much fun. Lou, you have the greatest attitude.

CPSIA information can be obtained
at www.ICGtesting.com
Printed in the USA
BVHW032340090521
606721BV00001B/44

9 781595 943828